Preface

These studies of Shakespeare in performance have a loose unity, that of my interests, but no agenda. I pursue essences and practices. Theatre history, as I view it, is less a fascinating study in itself than a means of knowing the plays. Through the record of performance, one sees what the plays *are*. Hence the shifting history of production tells us things about *Measure for Measure* and *The Tempest* (say) that we did not know a few years ago. Such studies are a provisional report on what we know now.

A changing angle of attack seems to me vital. Half of these studies deal with casting, the immediate 'how' of production. Directors will commonly say that 40–50 per cent of their success depends on casting, and yet the subject has not been obsessively studied. I touch here on some problems of doubling, on casting the chorus and the crowd, and on the star casting in *Hamlet* and *Measure for Measure*. The taming of the audience is the central challenge to all playwrights, and I analyse here some of Shakespeare's most original strategies. Cordelia, through her two asides, tells us what to think – for a while. The audience of *King Richard II* is encouraged through the subversive laughter of the piece to take another view of the action: there is a recurring possibility of the experience transforming itself into something quite different. With *The Tempest*, the transformations show up in the changing relationships between Prospero, Caliban and Ariel, a new model of the world we live in. The essence of *Henry IV* is a pastoral alternating with the world of duty. The scenic alternation of pleasure and duty is the basic programming of *Henry IV*, the way the staging affects us. Performance is the realization of identity.

Acknowledgements

I am indebted to the University of Ottawa for a research grant enabling me to complete this book. Four of its chapters have already been published, in *Shakespeare Quarterly*, *Assaph* and *Essays in Theatre*. The chapter on *Henry IV* was originally delivered as a paper to the Elizabethan Theatre conference at the University of Waterloo in 1987.

1

Hamlet's Doubles

In the RSC *Hamlet* of 1980, Michael Pennington's Hamlet, listening intently to the Player's account of Pyrrhus,

> So as a painted tyrant Pyrrhus stood,
> And, like a neutral to his will and matter . . .

anticipated the Player to complete the sentence himself:

> Did nothing.

> (2.2.476–78)

A bold touch, and perfectly in keeping with the play's echoic, self-referential quality. Everything that happens in *Hamlet* relates to the consciousness at the drama's centre; and Hamlet, with his supreme self-awareness, constantly sees in others images of himself. Laertes and Fortinbras are only the most obvious examples. The Player, in the passage cited, reminds Hamlet of what he knows, and would as soon forget.

Now this quality of *Hamlet* animates the doubling possibilities that are coded into the text. Given a company of 15–16, the assumed strength of the Chamberlain's Men, extensive doubling was inevitable. Full casting – a different actor for each part – was an indulgence of the Victorian/ Edwardian stage, a demonstration of lavish acting values. Most stages, and the provinces everywhere, have had to accommodate more austere castings. *Hamlet* is designed for productions in which actors appear and reappear in different guises, hauntingly reminding the audience of what was said and expressed earlier in similar voices, other habits.

What, in the most general sense, is the effect? A. C. Sprague distinguishes between deficiency doubling (together with emergency doubling) and virtuoso doubling.[1] The first variety is aimed simply at making good the numerical deficiencies of the company. Doubling has often been concealed (by such devices as 'Walter Plinge,' together with his American associate 'George Spelvin'), the management being ashamed to admit the company's limitations. It follows from this perception that the actor's triumph was to submerge himself, unrecognizably, in his several roles. The second variety, on the contrary, glories in a display of character acting. As Sprague and Trewin note, 'Polonius and one of the Gravediggers (most likely the First) . . . was once the most popular of all Shakespearian doubles.'[2] This double goes back to 1730, and Sprague, in the appendix to his monograph, lists many instances. Neither variety of doubling, I think, exists in the same form today. Deficiency doubling there must always be, but nobody is ashamed of it; the actors tackle their assignments openly. The concept of virtuoso doubling is scarcely mainstream, and the actor playing Polonius is unlikely to relish the implication that this is the first leg of a comic double. Poloniuses are usually praised for not overdoing the comic touches. Broadly, then: doubling is not a uniform mode, implying a single variety of audience response. It will depend on the circumstances and attitudes of the stage in its era. And a history of *Hamlet* doubling is well beyond my scope here. I want to examine, first, some aspects of the doubling problems which the text of *Hamlet* discloses; second, some solutions which theatrical practice, in London and Stratford-upon-Avon, has proposed in the past century. And finally, I will use these solutions to return to the nature of the text itself.

Shakespeare's two-part structures are fundamental to his dramaturgy. From *Richard III* to *The Winter's Tale*, there are numerous before-and-after compositions, some of them, like *Timon of Athens*, exceptionally clear-cut. The schema calls for a number of lower/middle-order parts, which will appear and disappear before the midpoint, whose actors can be re-deployed in the later stages of the play. It is a principle of organization, not a fixed plan of allocation. Shakespeare must be aware that the actor playing Strato will come from the pool containing Flavius, Marullus and Casca; the disposition of company forces can be made, without preconception, in the light of the available talents. The doubling charts that have been drawn up for *Richard II* and *Julius Caesar* show us how the thing was done.[3] The two-part structure accommodated the doubling that was basic to performances in Shakespeare's day, a practice, says G. E. Bentley, of which audiences were fully aware.[4]

Hamlet is not self-evidently a two-part structure, and commentators who assume such a structure have disputed whether the midpoint lies in the Play Scene or the Closet Scene. Nevertheless, the 'centred symmetry,' the careful structural balancing which Keith Brown adduces between the outer Acts cannot be gainsaid, and I find his 'centric view' of the larger Act 3 cogent. On Brown's showing, *Hamlet* is indeed symmetrical, but its midpoint is itself a 'central act' covering several scenes, with the play dividing into Acts 1–2; 3–4.3; and 4.4–5.[5] Suppose we apply this tripartite division to the doubling problem; it corresponds reasonably well to the challenges of organizing roles other than the major ones. The early stages of *Hamlet* require decent middle-order casting for Marcellus, Bernardo, Francisco, Voltemand, Cornelius, and Reynaldo. These parts disappear before the middle stages, which call upon Rosencrantz, Guildenstern, First Player (presumably, Player King), Player Queen, Prologue, Lucianus, Norwegian Captain, and Fortinbras. Fortinbras will be needed for the later stages, which also require two Gravediggers, Sailor, Priest, Osric, and English Ambassador. Without taking note of attendants, or such immediate possibilities as a conflation of Lucianus and Prologue, one sees at once that half-a-dozen decently capable actors are called for in the early stages, again in the middle, and again in the later stages of the play. They can accomplish their tasks in various permutations of tripling, which grow progressively less onerous as the cast numbers available move up between 6–7 and 20.

All this assumes a full text, or something like it. *Hamlet*, the quarry-text par excellence, invites cuts aimed at re-shaping the material (and not merely reducing the bulk). The major possibilities are too well known to need elaboration. Theatregoers today collect Reynaldos in the way their ancestors collected English Ambassadors and Fortinbrases. An assiduous but unscholarly Victorian/Edwardian play-goer might have imagined that *Hamlet* ends at 'And flights of angels sing thee to thy rest.' And in Olivier's film even Rosencrantz and Guildenstern found no place. Serious cutting, of the surgical order, finds it easy to eliminate parts as well as lines from *Hamlet*. This obvious but unpursuable fact I record and abandon. The discussion of doubling here takes for granted an approximation to a full text, whether of Folio or Second Quarto.

The complexity of this situation disposes of any idea that there can be a natural track whereby certain dispositions taken early on lead to 'convenient options' after the interval. Instead, the actors are conducted through the 'junction' of the mid-section – which, for our purposes, is the Play Scene – after which they are to be re-deployed in new and unpredictable ways. Let us take the opening scene as the simplest illustration of the problems. Three soldiers are required, in addition to Horatio and the Ghost. Of these, Francisco is the least substantial; he exits early, does not re-appear, and is available for recasting at all later points. Bernardo must remain throughout scene 1, and is with the group that announces the news of the Ghost to Hamlet in 1.2. Marcellus, the most important of the three, is additionally present in the battlement scenes of 1.4 and 1.5. Thereafter he, like his colleagues on watch, must return to the acting pool. From there he will emerge later in ways that defy prescription. The director may take the view (a) that Marcellus, having already had a reasonably substantial part, must now submit to something less distinguished, or (b) that Marcellus, an actor of some ability in a lean company, must be given something at least as good later on. Of the three on guard duty, the actor with the most soldierly bearing might be retained for Fortinbras; the second such, Norwegian Captain. How are parts re-assigned via the 'junction'? What is the previous existence of the Priest? Is a tripling feasible, or does the director save a part by combining Lucianus/Prologue, thus yielding a spare actor who could take over Francisco, always provided that Captain could return as Sailor, granted that English Ambassador is taken care of . . .? The combinations spin and re-form. Always the director is in the business of playing to strength and masking weakness, of trying to match numbers with burly sailors, soldierly soldiers, lizard-like courtiers and reverend priests, not to mention bloat kings and Gertrudes who are not too obviously younger than Hamlets. He must avoid being end-played with reverend soldiers or lizard-like sailors, unless, despairing, he resolves to defy stereotype. To arrive at pre-formed answers to these puzzles would seem beyond the wit of man.

Thus the text, as it discloses itself to initial reflection. Scene 1 is not in itself especially important as a casting problem. The director is likely to start elsewhere, from the perception that such a one is an ideal Osric and another is one of Nature's Guildensterns, and to build up his castings from that point. It is simply that scene 1 comes first, even if closed out late in the casting process. From it one can trace the network of options criss-crossing into a mathematical blur, as the tracks lead away from the apparent simplicities of Francisco, Bernardo, and Marcellus. They, too, have an identity problem. Who are they going to play next?

Hamlet will always be a Rubik's cube of the director's art. What can theatrical practice tell us about the solutions? Of the infinite mass of material available in theory, I select two major samplings as convenient and apt. J. P. Wearing's calendar of the London stage now extends from 1890 to 1929.[6] Michael Mullin's catalogue-index covers a century of productions in Stratford-upon-Avon (and latterly, London).[7] The cast lists, save for the remoter years in Stratford-upon-Avon, are reasonably full. Together, these catalogues cover a hundred productions of *Hamlet*. It is enough to stimulate generalization.

The main conclusion is marked. There is nothing approaching a central, continuing tradition of *Hamlet* doubling. Historic situations change, for one thing. The London stage, as I have mentioned, adopted a standard of lavish, full casting. In the entire Edwardian era, there were only a handful of doublings (most of them in Wearing, 09.14). One is startled to come across a doubling of Bernardo and the Ghost, but one's sense of hallucination fades with the knowledge that William Poel arranged the text (Wearing, 14.12). During the 1914–18 war years, certain exigencies were obviously forced upon managements. Even so, Martin Harvey at His Majesty's (Wearing, 16.93) kept alive Beerbohm Tree's practice of full casting. (Tree, in keeping with the opulent standards of his day, used to add a Court Jester to his cast.) After the war, Lilian Baylis's frugal reign at the Old Vic involved regular and frequent doubling. At Stratford-upon-Avon, Benson, of course, had to cut corners; and Bridges-Adams, operating under the fiscally conservative Sir Archibald Flower, had to deploy his forces with great care.

Since 1945 the Shakespeare Memorial Theatre, later the Royal Shakespeare Company, has generally been able to cast as it pleased. There was however a remarkable production in 1975 by the late Buzz Goodbody at The Other Place (Mullin, 0280) in which triple castings were normal. Charles Dance, for example, was well reviewed for the unlikely combination of Reynaldo, Third Player, and Fortinbras. Of recent years, doubling at Stratford-upon-Avon has reflected not exigencies but the director's wish to make a point. To that I shall return.

Conditions, though changing, do not I think generate historic trends in patterns of doubling. What one finds are odd pockets of practices, which turn out to reflect the taste of a director able to return over the years to *Hamlet*. Benson, for example, liked to cast Marcellus and First Player, irrespective of the actors available. Bridges-Adams favored the doubling of Ghost and Fortinbras, doing so on four occasions from 1920 to 1929. Robert Atkins, who directed five *Hamlets* in London during the early 1920s, four at the Old Vic, also experimented with Ghost/Fortinbras (twice). Tripling was common at the Old Vic during that era, and no one combination dominated. One finds Frances L. Sullivan combining Francisco/Priest/English Ambassador (Wearing, 22.117). To approach the matter from another angle, suppose we sample the doubles with which Bernardo was associated: the first four decades of this century at Stratford-upon-Avon yield us Guildenstern (twice); Second Player (four times); Priest; Rosencrantz (twice); Fortinbras; Second Gravedigger. London, from 1900–29, gives us Rosencrantz (three times); First Player (twice); Osric (twice); Second Gravedigger (twice); Priest; and Captain. It is tedious to demonstrate the obvious. Doubling practice in *Hamlet* is, and must always have been, overwhelmingly opportunistic.

A negative curiosity is worth mentioning. If we can be tolerably sure of any specific doubling in Shakespeare's own company, it is that of Marcellus and Voltemand. The First Quarto evidence seems to confirm an authentic practice of the Chamberlain's Men, that a single actor was responsible for Marcellus and Voltemand together with Prologue and Lucianus.[8] One might expect Marcellus/ Voltemand to be at least a cult double, a purist's double. I can find no evidence of its popularity, now or in any era. Voltemand is an early candidate for elimination, as the director eyes his options together with the playing-text; Voltemand's lot may well be to join the woebegone Cornelius in the limbo reserved for non-players. But that does not account for the continuing irrelevance of a doubling practice from Shakespeare's own company.

Theatre practice, then, reveals no consistent pattern of doublings. Polonius/Gravedigger had two centuries of esteem before fading. Even Ghost/Laertes was practised for a hundred years, an oddity which Sprague has preserved for us.[9] Individual directors have favoured or experimented with certain combinations. But there is no master key. The search for through lines yields only a crazy pattern of interconnected lines. One has then to accept that the play is like that: it is an infinitely complex set of possibilities, not a logical grid with well-defined paths.

A third variety of doublings I shall term 'conceptual.' This is a modern phenomenon. In conceptual doublings, the director looks beyond numbers, and beyond the physical characteristics of the acting corps, to couplings which have an underground linkage. Recognizing that the play's unity comprehends all its parts, the director wishes to italicize into a formal relationship two of them. Conceptual doubling brings a hidden relationship to light. Suppose we think of the play as a metro subway system, the characters as stations: to double parts with conceptual intent is to colour-code the stations on the subway map. The play's meaning as realized in performance is then held to depend, not minimally, on a relationship whose intensity the director

proposes. This tactic affords the director of *Hamlet* an especially inviting range of possibilities in those pairings which
include the Ghost.

The Ghost is the animating spirit of *Hamlet*. Everything
that happens in the play, from the initial 'Who's there?' is an
index of or reaction to this appearances. The play's subtitle
is an adjustment: 'Not the King of Denmark.' Admonishing
and dominating his son, the Ghost, like Julius Caesar, is
'mighty yet'; and young Hamlet, going through a series of
admissions and submissions that leads to the use of the
royal seal and the taking-up of arms, acknowledges his
kingly mentor. And yet the all-pervasiveness of the Ghost's
influence does not march with the actor's duties. Two silent
appearances in the opening scene, a major cadenza in 1.4–5,
a brief intervention in 3.4: it is not much for the play's
arbiter. Where else can the old mole re-emerge?

Peter Hall's *Hamlet* at the National Theatre (1975) offered
a clearcut illustration of a possible answer. The National,
operating to neo-Edwardian standards of luxury casting,
has not tended to economize on actors. One reviewer indeed compared disparagingly the large cast at the National
to the 14-strong RSC corps, then playing the Goodbody
Hamlet at the Round House.[10] In the National's production
(which contained *two* English Ambassadors) there was a
single major doubling: the Ghost and Claudius.

Everything a director does is liable to be construed as
reductionist, but this looks like a severe case. The linkage of
Ghost and Claudius is patently a homage to Freud, to Ernest
Jones's Freud anyway. According to Jones, 'The call of duty
to kill his stepfather cannot be obeyed because it links itself
with the unconscious call of his nature to kill his mother's
husband, whether this is the first or second; the absolute
repression of the former impulse involves the inner prohibi-
tion of the latter also.'[11] An earlier generation of directors –
Guthrie, say – might have put that quotation brazenly in
the programme. Hall was content to leave the audience to

draw its own conclusions. Vulgar Freudianism, which traditionally calls for an unseemly wrestling sequence between Gertrude and Hamlet on her bed, was thus rejected in favour of an understated gesture. Interested, the reviewers noted the doubling without hazarding an interpretation. 'Subsequent original details consist of Denis Quilley's doubling of Claudius and the Ghost (who, for once, is a suffering rather than an admonitory spectre)' is Irving Wardle's cautious phrasing.[12] 'Denis Quilley's booming, Wagnerian Ghost lays the revenge ball firmly in his son's court,' is Michael Coveney's.[13] 'It was an interesting idea to double the roles of Claudius and the Ghost,' says Robert Speaight, without however going on to expound the idea's interest.[14] Collectively, the reviewers were puzzled at Hamlet's failure to act, the more so as Albert Finney, a raw and virile presence, scarcely suggested Oedipal inhibition. The verdict on the experiment must be 'not proven.'

Yet Hall had tried it before, in the 1966 revival of his RSC production starring David Warner. Eric Shorter identifies 'the paternal Brewster Mason doing a Freudian double as Claudius and the Ghost.'[15] Mason's was a huge Ghost, towering over all; Hamlet would have to outgrow his parent. Thus the Ghost/Claudius double may be held to conflate a parent-figure, rather than promote a specifically sexual problem in Gertrude, Claudius, and Hamlet. Whatever the gloss, the Ghost/Claudius doubling was one that reviewers preferred to skirt around, in 1966 as in 1975. The idea remains essentially unproven and perhaps of dubious value. Practical directors, as Keynes might say, are slaves to some defunct critic.

I pass over with some reluctance the Ghost/Priest double, which Trevor Nunn experimented with in his RSC *Hamlet* (1970). That production was strongly imbued with religious values. Act 3, scene 1 was set in a chapel, and Hamlet left Orphelia slumped in a pew. Hamlet wore a black cowl from the Players' wardrobe in 3.3, as also in 4.2.

He was brought before Claudius in a cloister where black-cowled monks were gathered.[16] Was the Priest, then, a signal of reality after play-acting? There is a case for seeing the Priest as the reminder of what the Ghost had imparted to Hamlet. But none of the reviewers on file at the Stratford archives showed any interest in this doubling, and I prefer not to make out a theoretical case when its practice failed to make an impression on those who witnessed the production.

A much more important double has had a significant if inconclusive testing. Robert Speaight, in his autobiography, writes of the 1923 Angmering Festival: 'Gyles Isham had agreed to double the Ghost and Fortinbras – an excellent idea which I have never seen repeated.'[17] Speaight could in fact have seen the double in Stratford-upon-Avon and London during the 1920s, when it had something of a vogue. Bridges-Adams directed the play eight times at Stratford, four of them exploiting the Ghost/Fortinbras double (Mullin, 0259, 0262, 0263, 0264). The first occasion, in 1920, must be accounted a false cast. The visual appearance of the Ghost was left to the audience's imagination, to the displeasure of the reviewers. The *Daily News* remarked acidly that 'it is modernizing Shakespeare too much to omit the ghost and only to hear his voice. Apparently, Hamlet saw his father somewhere in the dress circle.'[18] From 1927 through 1929 Bridges-Adams tried again, this time giving the Ghost a corporeal presence. Gordon Bailey was the actor of the Ghost and Fortinbras in all three productions, evidently a satisfactory solution. In the 1927 production, the reviewers were well pleased with the Ghost's delivery, as also with the Hamlet of John Laurie and the Ophelia of Lydia Sherwood. In the following seasons, Bailey's distinctive and memorable Ghost continued to be singled out for praise. 'His voice is remarkably good, reaching a note at the final "Remember me" which moves one deeply and creates the feeling of suspense which is so vital at this point.'[19] And: 'A special

word of praise is due to Mr. Gordon Bailey's Ghost, a really
impressive figure in spite of those persistent grey draperies.
Does Mr. Bridges-Adams really think the King wore an old
wedding-veil when he smote the sledded Polacks on the
ice?'[20] The last point makes all clear. Bailey's Ghost had no
face, but a presence and a voice; he transmitted his identity
to Fortinbras as a vocal echo. What Fortinbras received as
his genetic heritage from the Ghost was a distinctive and
memorable voice.

In London, Robert Atkins more or less had the *Hamlet*
concession during the 1920s. His Old Vic productions were
well-regarded, offering successively Ernest Milton, Russell
Thorndike, and Ion Swinley in the title role. Twice, Atkin
doubled the Ghost with Fortinbras: first with Austin Trevor,
then with Stephen Jack (Wearing, 22.117 and 25.112). These
productions received few reviews, and *The Stage* and *The
Era* have nothing of consequence to say. *The Times* was
frankly gravelled: 'It is difficult to understand the motives
which have prompted the Old Vic's interpretation of the
ghost – an overpowering Ghost, as pompous as Polonius
and without Polonius's variety, in mind and form a most
substantial Ghost.'[21] Another inconclusive experiment, it
would seem. But Atkins must have had in mind the concept
of a dominating Ghost, emerging into action as Fortinbras.
Latterly the point has been made more clearly, in the
practice of Jonathan Miller. For his production at The
Warehouse (1982), he had Philip Locke double the Ghost
and Player King. As Miller explained in an interview: 'In
the first production I did I tripled: Player King, Ghost,
and Fortinbras, because these were the three models of
decisiveness and vigour with which Hamlet unfavorably
compares himself.'[22]

The logical terminus to this line of thought is the doubling of Hamlet and the Ghost. This, the most extreme possibility in Ghost doubling, was tested in Richard Eyre's
production at the Royal Court (April 1980). 'There is no

Ghost in this production. Jonathan Pryce, in what is effectively his first soliloquy, plays both sides of the conversation between Hamlet and his dead father, adopting for the latter a deep voice wrenched from his stomach despite himself, causing considerable physical contortion.'[23] The first scene was cut, and Hamlet's encounter with his father's spirit did not occur until 1.5. 'Instead of receiving the demand for revenge from his dead father, Hamlet, pronounces it himself while in a state of apparent "possession".'[24] Illegitimate, of course. And yet the reviewers did not register a collective sense of outrage at the text's being violated. In part, their reaction was a tribute to Jonathan Pryce's acting, a performance of great intensity and power. 'His body convulsed, eyes closed, head rocking back, Pryce belches up the Ghost's word from the depths of his stomach in an agonizing howl. It is a spectacular and mesmerizing effect that completely overshadows the substance of the words themselves, but introduces a sense of mystery and power fully in tune with the animal vigour of the Prince.'[25] In part, it was an admission of exorcism as a then fashionable topic. But the reviewers also sensed a certain legitimacy in the director's tactic, stemming from the perception that the Ghost does in some way speak through Hamlet, that the double is a primal conflation of two shelves.

The doubling of the Ghost and Hamlet crystallizes the underground logic of the play. Everything in *Hamlet* has the potential to bear upon the play's centre, to offer a broken *samizdat* on Hamlet's consciousness. This potential could not have been realized in the performances of Shakespeare's day. There, the needs of repertory and a limited company (15–16) would have severely limited casual experimentation. Further, the conceptual doubling which reveals the play's underground logic depends upon a director, a functionary with no existence in England until the late nineteenth century. Thus the multiple possibilities within the text have had to await testing in the subsequent history of *Hamlet* in performance. The doublings of stage history offer a mechanistic parallel to the castings of, and within, Hamlet. Conceptual doubling, a twentieth century development, assumes a company of reasonable numbers and resources, and a director who is perceived to be making significant choices in his castings. Within this tradition, a line of modern directors from Bridges-Adams to Jonathan Miller and Richard Eyre has, I think, filed a major claim on *Hamlet*. It is this: doubling, executed with intent beyond the older categories of emergency and virtuoso, can express a ruling perception of the text's values. In the end, the possibilities within the great play, social and genetic, can be reduced to a single likeness (Hamlet/Hamlet), a single admonition ('Remember'), a single acknowledgement. The Ghost's pairings all aspire to the selves of Hamlet. And the last double, as the stage now proposes, is that of Hamlet and his father.

2
Doubling: Theory and Practice

The theory of Shakespearean doubling cannot be confined to the record of stage practice. Many doubles have stage sanction; some have been tried on stage, but are obviously useless (Ghost/Laertes, Falstaff/Henry IV)[1]; many more doubles are theoretically feasible and reflect interesting possibilities in the text. Such conceptual doubles are distinct from inert or routine doubles. It is of no consequence to know whether Flavius or Marullus is told off to learn Strato's lines. And Shakespeare's two-part structures constantly create new roles for the actors, many of which have no special interest when linked with other roles. But subterranean linkage between characters, and with it the experimental possibility of doubling, is inherent in Shakespearean drama. The stage's experiments can at least initiate thought, and perhaps demonstrate conclusion.

I begin with a double that has, I think, surfaced after a long period of neglect. The 1988 season at Stratford, Ontario offered a *Richard III* in which Geraint Wyn Davies played King Edward IV and Richmond. As soon as the double is proposed, one sees the point: the Sick King yields to the New King, a death is followed by a rebirth. There is a certain textual balancing to the roles, for while Spevack gives Richmond twice as many words as Edward, the number of speeches is almost even (twelve to Edward, fourteen to Richmond). Edward and Richmond are of approximating mass in the play's structure, and this can be conveniently realized on stage, for each part looks to be of 'hired man' status. F. R. Benson, who liked to vary his doubles over the years, tried it out with Baliol Holloway at Stratford-upon-Avon (1912) and again with Charles Warburton (1915).[2] In 1925 at the Old Vic, Andrew Leigh assigned the double to Geoffrey Wardwell.[3] What did the reviewers make of it? No reviews of the Benson productions survive in the Stratford archive, but J. P. Wearing has located seven of the Old Vic production. Most of them pass over the double with a perfunctory comment, or none. Even Agate in the *Sunday Times*, with space and means, ignored Wardwell.[4] But *The Stage* praised 'the picturesquely romantic Richmond of Mr Geoffrey Wardwell . . . Mr Wardwell previously doubled the rather lachrymosely presented and preciously spoken moribund Edward IV.'[5] Clearly, the reviewer saw no more than a simple contrast here, a minor example of deficiency/virtuoso doubling, not a 'concept.' For a 'concept,' one needs a climate of opinion in which the director's choice is perceived as interesting and significant. This climate, which exists today, did not, or not to the same degree, in the 1920s. Hence the Edward IV/ Richmond double means something different in 1925 and 1988. In the past, we can see no more than the reviewers saw, which is a contrasted double turn. It strikes me as a Hired Man's Prize Song for entry into the sharers. In the recent instance, we are to follow the director's line of thought and meditate on a fruitful connection. Whatever the circumstances of performance, the double seems a perfectly feasible way of pointing up Shakespeare's design.

This can hardly be said of the much-discussed Cordelia/ Fool double. There is no question of the numerous structural links between Cordelia and the Fool, which are canvassed by Thomas B. Stroup.[6] Each is the teller of truth, the mirror, as Derek Traversi says, of Lear's consciousness. There is a kind of mental convergence between them in Lear's eyes. In Stroup's trenchant phrase, 'Cordelia and the Fool function as one character . . . they serve merely as one component force.' But one can still doubt Stroup's conclusion, that the structural links strengthen the likelihood of a double. It seems likelier that the two parts should be played by separate individuals (even if, historically, we can make out a case via Robert Armin's small stature and versatility). They are, after all, serious major parts. W. J. Lawrence thought that the sharers, that is, those commanding the major parts in Shakespeare's company, 'disdained doubling'. The Cordelia/Fool double he found 'difficult to swallow. Proof that leading female characters were ever doubled is wholly lacking.'[7] William A. Ringler held that Armin probably did not play the Fool: the role was doubled with Cordelia, he thought, by the leading boy actor.[8] But David Wiles takes it for granted that Armin played the Fool,[9] and it seems inherently probable that Armin exercised territorial rights over the role. Would the 'allowed fool' of the company yield his part to a boy, in a tragic masterpiece? Everything we know about Armin suggests that he fought his corner. Thus the problem of double casting must have been difficult, perhaps intractable in Shakespeare's day. Later stage practice has not been attracted to the Cordelia/Fool double. It strikes me as a rather academic fancy, based on the premise that because a double is technically possible it is worth doing. One cannot erect a multi-storey edifice on the bald fact that two characters never meet on stage.

A parallel case is the linkage of Cloten and Posthumus. 'I cannot delve him to the root,' but the idea of this double has been around for some time. In Komisarjevsky's last production, *Cymbeline* (Montreal, 1950), the organizer, Rosanna Seaborn Todd, pressed the idea upon him. Komisarjevsky responded negatively, and a letter of his on file at the McCord Museum, Montreal, puts his views on record. 'I was very interested in your suggestions, though I am quite sure that Posthumus and Cloten have to be played by different actors, bodily alike, but facially and mentally different.'[10] On the level of stage-craft, Komisarjevsky is obviously right. And yet, it is clear that Shakespeare thinks of Imogen's

suitors as some sort of dramatic equation: gentleman and
oaf, the meritocrat and the high-born booby. These characteristics are not exclusive to each role. Posthumus behaves
badly, and Cloten has one speech, 'You sin against/Obedi-
ence' (2.4), which has the accent of intelligence and realistic
worldly judgment. The qualities are commingled: there is a
leakage from one compartment to another. In addition, the
play offers a disquisition on clothes and the man, with the
headless corpse as an outré visual pun. These matters are
easy to write about, but it would be pointless to illustrate
them through the same actor; the effect would be at best
heavy and didactic.[11] (The Colonel's Lady and Judy O'Grady
is not an ideal double.) The 'double' here is merely a way of
thinking about Shakespeare's methods of constructing a
play.

The same point emerges with greater force in the linkage
of Autolycus and Leontes. 'Autolycus,' remarks Joan
Hartwig, 'is both his own attacker and victim; so is Leontes.'
More broadly, 'Autolycus thus absorbs some of the dis-
ordering aspects of Leontes' disturbed imagination from
the first half of the play.'[12] Autolycus ['self-wolf'] exorcizes
the sickness in Leontes; he is the spirit of comedy who takes
over from tragedy. More, the Autolycus/Leontes pairing
contains an odd hint of the Edward IV-Richmond double.
Autolycus' first song contains subliminal hints of a New
King. 'For the red blood *reigns* in the winter's pale . . . For a
quart of ale is a dish for a *king*.' This song is not only a
celebration of Spring, but a muted acknowledgement of
the Sick King whose passing is complete in Act 3. Act 4 sees
the larger comedy break through the carapace of tragedy
(whose resistance it has been testing from at least 2.3 on).
The agent of that comedy is Autolycus, who must however
be decorously absent from the final scene of *The Winter's
Tale*. The roles of Autolycus and Leontes are plain enough,
and the play's end sees the New King as the Restored King.
But comedy and tragedy do not meet face to face.

All this can be argued in greater detail.[13] And yet, a Leontes/Autolycus double is all but inconceivable (save for a company of severely limited numbers). There is no stage history of the double, to my knowledge. It would throw a great burden on the actor. And there is an awkward transition when Autolycus exits at the end of Act 4 and Leontes enters at the beginning of Act 5. A double would be a sterile exercise in virtuosity, like the Falstaff/Henry IV feat cited earlier. The effect would be of an actor on steroids lifting excessive weights. One would rather see two human beings entertaining us in individual ways.

Every case has to be judged on its merits. There is no rule that I can discover beyond the general tendency for major roles to exclude other roles. A natural candidate for appraisal is the most celebrated Shakespearean double of the past, Polonius and First Gravedigger. This, Sprague's 'virtuoso' double,[14] has now largely disappeared from the stage. Poloniuses do not see themselves as the first leg of a comic double. These days, actors prefer to stress Polonius as wise elder statesman, kindly paterfamilias, unhappy victim of the maniac Hamlet. They like to harvest press notices in which the reviewer commends Polonius for being no kind of buffoon (as though anyone has ever seen a buffoon Polonius in recent memory). They disown any kind of kinship with the Gravedigger, an embarrassing cadet branch of the house. And yet, as one looks at the Polonius/Gravedigger parallels, a kind of blowsy affinity emerges. There is the same yearning for the role of Wise Man, and the same penchant for linguistic games. Each is desperate for an audience. The Gravedigger is Polonius without the social advantages, and if an actor cares to bring out the affinities, why not? It is no more than playing the caricature besides the straight sketch. The double is consecutive, not interlinked.

Polonius does an encore, by popular demand. And if this is held to distort the contours of Polonius, we have, after all, good authority for classifying Polonius among 'These tedious old fools.' As to the double's practical utility, one rarely gets a chance to judge; but I took in Ingmar Bergman's production for the Royal Swedish Theatre (National Theatre, 1987), where Ulf Johanson offered a discreetly shaded comic Polonius (and Gravedigger), well in line with the gamey and derisive vista on the Danish court which the Swedish directed or proposed. I left with the distinct impression that there is more to be said for the Polonius/Gravedigger double than current practice on the English stage admits. Still, the main principle is no doubt intact: if one has available a Felix Aylmer-type and a Stanley Holloway-type actor available, one does best to cast them as Polonius and Gravedigger.

If there is a conventional Shakespearean double on today's stage, it is Theseus/Oberon and Hippolyta/Titania. This has been popular since Peter Brook launched the fashion, in his RSC (1970) production. One should not direct, Brook reasoned, as though there were three different worlds: 'The more one examines the play, the more one sees how these worlds interweave.'[15] Irving Wardle echoed this view: 'We are accustomed to seeing them as inhabitants of different worlds. Brook shows them as members of the same world.'[16] But the reviewers found little to interest them in the psychological aspects of the doubling, and Benedict Nightingale declared roundly that 'there's more doubling of the kind, for no real reason except economy.'[17] The widespread doubling, which extended to Egeus/Quince and Philostrate/Puck, may have blurred its own impact. Still, the double of the four leads has continued to fascinate directors, who find I think a different meaning in it than did Brook. What emerges in recent productions is a sense of the emotional tensions between the lead actors, in both roles.

Structurally, the case to be made out is easy. The *Dream* offers a study in pre-marital and post-marital tensions. The early apprehensions and reservations of Hippolyta (which is not a new concept; one can see it in Reinhardt's film) foreshadow the open jealousies and resentments of the fairy rulers: 'We are their parents and original.' The twin relationships are sequential in marital time, and bombard each other with particles of meaning. There may be, for example, a shadowy quartet of alter-ego role players, such as are reduced to two in Pinter's *The Lover*. There is even a custody battle, not so far from the emotional arena of *Kramer vs Kramer*. All this can be picked up by actors of intelligence and authority, prepared to let one part 'bleed' into the other. (And not, of course, to seal off the two parts.) Of recent years, the twin double has been mined for meaning by Ron Daniels for the RSC (1981) and in two major productions at Stratford, Ontario. Robin Phillips (1977) assigned Hippolyta/Titania to Maggie Smith, and Theseus/Oberon to Barry MacGregor. This was an oddly feminist line, with a wistful Hippolyta as the sexual and political thrall to a brutally masculine Theseus (who, at the end, stalked off stage alone; Hippolyta would have no choice but to follow him). The turbulence of the fairy relationship offered no sort of consolation. In 1984, John Hirsch gave the leads to Nicholas Pennell and Patricia Conolly, representing the basic debate between the male and female principles. What stood out, both on stage and in the Festival publicity, was the fairy component. Oberon was jealous, revengeful, manipulative, the dark side of the male psyche. Titania was vixenish and bitter, one who intensified the resentments felt by the captive Hippolyta (whose defeat was announced in a prologue-masque depicting Amazons and Athenians at war). Clearly, this parsing of sex differed radically from Brook's, who held that the *Dream* was above all a celebration of sex. Either way, the doubling schema must contribute to this sense of the play. Amongst recent curiosa of the genre I add the RSC (1986) production of Bill Alexander's, who doubled Hippolyta/Titania (Janet McTeer) but not Theseus/Oberon: hence the sexual groundplan was one woman, two men.

(Three, actually, since Hippolyta's revenge directed her towards the rough trade, Bottom.) This engaging *concetto* was abandoned in the Barbican transfer. All these variations stem from a single and highly defensible principle, that Oberon is the alter ego of Theseus, as is Titania of Hippolyta.

Even so, the objection raised by John Russell Brown to Brook's method remains on the table.

> Hippolyta and Titania, Theseus and Oberon, are openly doubled as if the actors' task was to make what likeness exists between the pairs as obvious and inescapable as possible, and to minimize the very considerable differences.[18]

I think this a telling criticism, which must naturally be stronger in certain plays than in others. Doubling exploits likeness. What of unlikeness, that obstinate particularity which is true of all human beings and is true of all Shakespearean roles?

The question raises awkward local questions, and I would prefer to answer it strategically. It would I think be generally agreed that the later Shakespeare is much less interested in the nuance of individual psychology than is the Shakespeare of the early and middle periods. The author of the final romances seems to meditate on types, the larger roles through which humanity must express itself. The relative filtering of individuality from, say, Ferdinand and Perdita gives an accurate sense of the direction in which Shakespeare is moving. Hence doubling becomes, it seems to me, more apt as expressive of the basic content of the romances. The key instance for inquiry is *Pericles*.

———

The underground linkages between parts may well be explored by a company with limited numerical strength. And here, the recent practice of Cheek by Jowl offers a line on the problems of casting *Pericles*. This play is peculiarly interesting in the doubling possibilities it contains, options which seem inherent in the text rather than the expedients to which a hard-pressed company is reduced. Marion Lomax notes that Cheek by Jowl performed *Pericles* (1984–85, directed by Declan Donnellan and Nick Ormerod) 'with a minimum of properties and only very basic distinguishing costumes: Thaisa and Dionyza were played by the same actress, Sadie Shimmin, contrasting real mother and evil guardian.'[19] The good/evil double was repeated by Amanda Harris, as Marina and the unnamed daughter of Antiochus. That is one way of distributing the female parts. Another way is suggested by Gary Taylor, whose study of the *Pericles* transmission argues that the text was reported by a boy actor who doubled Lychorida and Marina.[20] Ultz's production at the Theatre Royal, Stratford (1983) offered a variation in which Felicity Dean doubled Thaisa and Marina, while Darlene Johnson doubled Dionyza and the Act 5 Thaisa. The Thaisa/Marina double illustrates the grand perception of *The Winter's Tale*, that life is a series of roles based primarily on age. In *Pericles* especially, the act of doubling comes to suggest the dramatizing of aspects of the self.

Another line on *Pericles* comes through in the Stratford, Ontario production of 1986, directed by Richard Ouzounian. In this, Antiochus and Boult were played by Nicholas Pennell. At one level, this is simply an intelligent decision to utilize the services of the company's leading classical actor, on the very large Festival Stage (seating some 2200). On another, the casting focuses the text. Evil that is masked in Antiochus becomes open, explicit in Boult; what is veiled and tragically serious becomes transposed into a key of black comedy. Boult is what Antiochus becomes. There is a real point to retaining the same actor here, as the comedy's vector.

All these productions of *Pericles* derive from that of Terry Hands (RSC, 1969), which was based on the doubling principle. With main-theatre RSC doubling is a concept, not an expedient. The rationale was spelt out in Terry Hands's first talk to the cast, reproduced in the programme:

> We have no established precedent for doubling in *Pericles*, but equally the play does not suggest a naturalistic treatment: there is little attempt to change the language or idiom for each different country, and textually we are given no scenic detail. We are more aware of what is done in each place, than of the place itself. Similarly with the characters, they are what they do. Shakespeare's method appears to avoid peripheral involvement in order to focus on Pericles himself. This suggests a pattern which may be more fully realized by deliberate doubling. Firstly by Gower calling on a group of actors to tell his story, and secondly by linking those characters that specifically relate to Pericles himself. Thus it becomes possible to double Antiochus with Boult, Thaliard with Leonine, Cleon with the Pandar, Gower with Helicanus, Dionyza with the Bawd, and Thaisa with Marina.

These doubles are of differing kinds. Antiochus/Boult, as we have seen, offers masked and open evil; so does Dionyza/Bawd. Thaliard and Leonine are variations on the servant with orders to kill, Thaliard having his comic side. Cleon/Pandar is good/evil. Thaisa/Marina is youth/age/youth. They appear together in the final scene, but Marina does not speak and the staging problem is easily overcome. (The Thaisa/Marina pairing anticipates the last scene of *The Winter's Tale*. Since both Hermione and Perdita have active speaking parts, the double is much harder to bring off, though the RSC has tried it more than once: in 1969–70 [Judi Dench] and 1986–87 [Penny Downie].[21]) Gower might seem to stand alone, but in fact the baton passes to Helicanus in 2.4 with his speech, quite in the Gower vein, on the passing of Antiochus and his daughter. This double allows the presenter to wander in and out of the action, a stratagem often favored by directors who, by keeping Chorus on-stage, remind the audience of his mental presence. (Cf. the Chorus in Adrian Noble's *Henry V* [RSC, 1984–85] and Revenge in Michael Bogdanov's *The Spanish Tragedy* [National Theatre, 1983].) There is no single type of doubling in Hands's *Pericles*. It is a principle with several variants.

The effect of these doubles, in which the actors were easily recognized, is harder to analyse. There is no problem at the stylistic level. 'All this serves to hold naturalism at bay,' remarked Irving Wardle.[22] B. A. Young elaborates: 'There's a hieratic quality about all the acting, perfectly consistent with Mr Hands's conception of the play, but a handicap to anything ambitious in the way of characterization.'[23] And Benedict Nightingale: 'other actors, too, change parts without bothering to disguise their faces . . . Thus we're never allowed to forget that we're watching a masquerade, not an imitation of life.'[24] This seems an accurate appraisal. But much hinges on what I take to be the key double, Susan Fleetwood's Marina/Thaisa. 'I am really the same person all the time and we hope that at the end she becomes one ready to be joined with Pericles.'[25] B. A. Young referred to 'Susan Fleetwood, who doubles Thaisa with Marina too closely for comfort . . .' And Harold Hobson, ever the most forthright of reviewers, accentuated Young's note of unease: 'the subliminal impression (very important in this production) is that Pericles is in danger of misbehaving with his own child.'[26] Hobson wondered if this was indeed the director's intention, and one may well take it as an unwanted by-product of the doubling strategy rather than a willed effect. But it could not be discounted as illegitimate in a play saturated with the awareness of incest.

The dreamlike, hieratic quality of Hands's *Pericles* evidently rested upon its doubling, not all of which has been listed here.[27] At the heart of such doubling is the idea that the self is divided,[28] and that through the mechanisms of twinning and doubling we realize ourselves. Trevor Nunn, in his programme note, made this the theme of the play: '*Pericles* is a journey from the bestiality of Antiochus' Court to the temple of Diana. It is a metaphysical journey, rest only comes with self-knowledge.' This *Pericles* was an adaptation of the ideas mechanized in *The Comedy of Errors*.

To sum up. I know of no case where a specific double in Shakespeare is marked, that is, where the text seems to call unmistakably for the same actor to play two specified parts. There are innumerable opportunities, which are not however prescriptive, for Sprague's categories of virtuoso, emergency, and deficiency doubles. To them I add conceptual doubles, in which the director chooses to italicize the kinship between two parts. But this statement of affinity can rest on differing values and polarities. The second part may be basically similar to the first, or opposed, or complementary (youth/age, good/evil, positive/negative, comic/tragic, funny/serious). Hence it is usually possible to re-form the doubling options into a new kaleidoscope. The decision will always hinge on the numbers and individual qualities of the available cast.

Doubling, in the end, is what happens. It is the stage record of decisions that embody the possibilities within the text, the echoic and formal relations between parts. These possibilities are fluid, metamorphic. They are not prescriptively binding upon the director. If we feel for a general principle underlying all this, it may well come down to Stoppard's view of 'every exit being an entrance somewhere else.' A current is switched off, and later on. It might be simplest to think of doubling as symbiosis: or as death and rebirth.

3

Casting the Chorus

Chorus is normally an affair of doubling. Gower can usually, not always, look forward to an unshared part; Chorus in *Henry V*, always. But all other Shakespearean choruses and prologues are luxury castings for individual actors, which depend upon spacious production values. Certainly in Shakespeare's day, and very generally since, the actor playing chorus will have had to combine it with at least one other part. This double will be visible, so to speak; the actor does not disguise himself as chorus; there is a transference of playing values, and the identity of the linked part has at least the possibility of inflecting chorus. We ought to know chorus's subterranean partner, his stage sibling, and draw whatever conclusions we can.

These will often be banal. Chorus ought to speak the lines well, and the stage record makes it clear that a well-graced middle-order actor is often assigned the lines on those grounds. No other gloss is necessary. But even in these cases, one can often glimpse a vestigial concept in the double. Take *Romeo and Juliet*. It is a reasonable tactic to double Chorus and Prince. The Prince, on the usual Shakespearean model, *is* Verona; he knows what the play knows, and has the play's final ('choric') lines anyway. There is plenty of stage evidence for this approach. For example, the distinguished presence of Anthony Nicholls covered Chorus and Prince at Stratford-upon-Avon in 1958. That was Glen Byam Shaw's production, and Peter Hall, in the same theatre, adopted the double with Tony Church in 1961. There is no tension here between society's Governor and the choric spokesman, there is identity. The prospect of this tension is however central to the theory of chorus, and one is led back to Greek drama for the classic codings of the tension.

———————

Chorus, in William Arrowsmith's words, 'remained the conservative soul of the play, the articulate spokesman for traditional religion and society . . . For the chorus attends the action as a dependent society in miniature, giving the public resonance of individual action.'[1] This is easily done and easily understood. The main issue emerges in Arrowsmith's warning: 'But almost never is the chorus' judgment of events authoritative; it is an intruded voice, it is normally the voice of tradition, not the dramatist.' This, written of Greek drama, is the necessary preliminary to the Elizabethan chorus, and is tellingly true of the Chorus in *Doctor Faustus*. In this tension between the traditional voice and the dramatist's lies the essence of the play. How far does Marlowe go along with 'Whose fiendful fortune may exhort the wise/Only to wonder at unlawful things'? Hence the search for this tension is the key line into the choric issues.

Romeo and Juliet, as we have seen, is an easy instance of standard casting procedures. Montague or the Prince will do neatly as the choric twin. But this play is a primitive for our purposes. *Romeo and Juliet* is not, so to speak, an 'intelligent' play; it is totally unlike the intelligence-loaded *Julius Caesar* or *Troilus and Cressida*. Nobody in Verona seems to understand what is going on; nobody is capable of acting as raisonneur, and the Prince, who is better placed than anyone else, merely takes the line that brawling in the streets is a bad thing. So it is. But at this intellectual level, it would be absurd to speak of any kind of tension between differing views of the action. In any case, what kind of comment on the action could we supply, from our own vantage? Could we communicate with the actors, we would say: 'Don't be so hasty; sleep on it; be like the Venetians.' And this would be good advice, but would scarcely transform the intellectual mode of the play. *Romeo and Juliet* is a play where we can hardly claim to know better than the chorus; the conflicts on stage are literal and physical, not intellectual. At the play's end we might as well agree with the Prince/ Chorus, 'For never was a story of more woe,/Than this of Juliet and her Romeo.' What is the alternative?

Henry V is a galactic distance from *Romeo and Juliet*. Here, the choric tension is everywhere, and there are two ways of formulating it. First, one can say that there is an obvious gap between chorus and play. On the one hand the official spokesman for the Ministry of Defence, holding an admiring and indeed sycophantic mirror to Henry's military virtues. On the other hand, the 'real' action: prelates buying off the nationalization of church property with a well-timed war subsidy, traitors in high places, criminal riff-raff in low places (whose resemblance to soccer hooligans is faithfully noted in the English Shakespeare Company production), battle scenes that evoke the Somme and Vietnam. On this approach, the confident cheerleading of Chorus, and the grainy, matt realism of the events, is jarring. The play is balanced between the claims of Chorus and the claims of the action. But second, one can argue that this bifold awareness is located in Chorus, not just between him and his surroundings. In the old days Chorus was never ironic; he approved of all he beheld, or said he did. Nowadays the ironic Chorus is, if not a cliché, at least a respectable and familiar stage presence.

This goes back to the the 1960s, and the coming of the contemporary *Henry V*. (The 1950s were the aftermath of the Second World War, and Richard Burton's Henry at the Old Vic, 1955, was still in the Olivier mode.) A milestone was Michael Langham's production at Stratford, Ontario (1966), when William Hutt as Chorus released his great talent for irony. Chorus evidently had his reservations about the war, and spoke his lines in a detached, fairly sardonic

tone. 'Throughout the play he explains those vaulting odes
to imagination like a finger-wagging schoolmaster,' reported
Brooks Atkinson.[2] More emphatically, Ian McDiarmid's
Chorus for Adrian Noble's *Henry V* (RSC, 1984), a production which the director termed 'post-Falklands,' milked the
lines for heavy irony. And it is surprising how much they
can yield. When, for example, McDiarmid seized upon 'some
petty and unprofitable *dukedoms*!' one caught the malicious,
gleeful paradox in the word: it is impossible for a title
linked with broad lands to be anything but highly profitable. The question becomes, how much does the Chorus in
Henry V know? He may be permitted to know a great deal
– as much as the director knows, as much as the audience
knows. Or he may indicate that while he has some private
reservations, he has a job to do (like Mountjoy) and prefers,
on the whole, to keep his thoughts to himself. In the late
twentieth century it is not, I imagine, possible for Chorus to
return to the older mode and suppress all sense of reservation. Chorus may well these days opt for a mediating strategy, like Derek Jacobi in Kenneth Branagh's film of *Henry V*
(1989). That is, he will position himself on what I take to be
the formula for today's *Henry V*: it is a great war play
embedded in a greater anti-war play.

The casting and playing of the *Henry V* Chorus is a unique
problem in the canon. There is no other instance of a choric
casting which bears the entire weight of the director's view
of the play. It is however normal for chorus to express the
decorum of the production, the 'soul' of the piece, through
an astute doubling. *Henry VIII* is a neat, schematic instance.
Tyrone Guthrie (Stratford-upon-Avon, 1949) gave the Prologue to the Old Lady – a gossipy, sympathetic observer of
the action. As Muriel St Clare Byrne saw it, 'The Prologue
was spoken by the Old Lady, Anne Bullen's friend (Wynne
Clark) – a sound device to associate its serious and pertinent
comment with the theme of Tudor accession which is responsible for the structure of the whole play.'[3] She was 'a

perfect Holbein portrait.' At Stratford, Ontario (1986), Brian Rintoul assigned the lines to three courtiers, fearful lest their words miscarry to Henry.[4] That watchful tyrant was shown as paying close attention to the words of his subjects. Now these castings reflect two views of the play, which are accepted by scholars as the major generic alternatives. Guthrie, following Wilson Knight, saw *Henry VIII* as a historical romance. The scenes of pageantry and display present the action as a positive and benign historic progress. Rintoul, on the other hand, saw *Henry VIII* as a history in the way that *Henry V* is a history: it is a drama of political realism, in which a wilful and ruthless King crushes all opposition. The play's final words offer a romance, the birth of the great Elizabeth; the unstated event is a tragedy, the coming disgrace and execution of Elizabeth's mother, Anne Boleyn. The play knows more than it says. Thus the casting of the Chorus is the lead in to the director's choice of genre, romance or history.[5]

Troilus and Cressida is probably an easy choice for the director nowadays. In theory, one can assign the Prologue to a range of parts, including Agamemnon and Diomedes. He is 'armed, but not in confidence.' In practice, directors choose Thersites, or not. The RSC productions of the 1970s and 1980s (directed by John Barton and Terry Hands) made Thersites the voice of the play, whether or not he spoke the lines: the production (and indeed the programme) proclaimed that 'All the argument is a cuckold and a whore.' That was Barton's production of 1976, one that stood solidly behind Thersites (and also, his view of Cressida). Barton, and later Hands, chose to ignore the play's tension between chivalric values and their challenge, and presented a full-frontal anti-Establishment lampoon, in which Thersites drowned the opposition. Keith Hack (OUDS, 1977) went further, in assigning Prologue to Thersites. Thersites, played by Tim McInnerny, was a wounded soldier, limping along with a combined bandage and crutch slung under one leg.

This shell-shocked figure, spokesman for the war's losers, was on stage for much of the time. Against him was Helen, visible for *all* the time; she was suspended above the action, swinging langorously and preening herself in a looking-glass. This icon of vapid beauty looked down on the choric soldier – who had fought for her. This was an extreme but defensible director's schema. But Howard Davies (RSC, 1985), eccentrically, gave the Prologue's lines to a Servant/ Waiter, bringing the tourist Pandarus up to date with the local news: 'In Troy,' he explained, 'there lies our scene,' information which Pandarus, struggling with a Balkans newspaper, seemed relieved to obtain. But these are minor *scherzi*. The casting of Prologue has still not received definitive treatment in modern productions of the RSC, and the easy linkage with Thersites is chosen as a serviceable exit from the problems.

To these 'decorum' castings of Chorus I add Olivier's production of Ford's *The Broken Heart* (Chichester, 1962). Olivier played Bassanes, and also spoke Prologue and Epilogue. T. J. B. Spencer, in his Revels edition of the play, quoted the *Times* review of 11 July 1962: 'In the hands of Sir Laurence, Bassanes, the unwanted husband, is raised to almost excessive authority, as if through this survivor of the killings we are to see the reality behind the stoical poses of the others.'[6] Prologue spoke his lines from the upper stage, and the unique authority of Olivier – inflected, perhaps, by the events of his private life – dominated the production. Again, Sir John Gielgud, who played Sir Politick Wouldbe in Peter Hall's production of *Volpone* (National Theatre, 1978), spoke Prologue's lines. The witty, urbane phrasing conveyed the voice, but not the mind, of Sir Politick. All schemata aside, it is simply a good idea to let a great actor speak the Prologue.

The Winter's Tale offers some intriguing variations on the choric double. Time, as everyone agrees, is the soul of the play; he has however a single speech only, at the beginning of Part Two, and this is dispensable. One learns from Denis Bartholomeusz's stage history that Kemble cut out Time completely, as did Macready and Phelps. 'Time, who is at the heart of the play's mystery, was not a character in the play on stage in the first half of the nineteenth century.'[7] Charles Kean restored Time in 1856, a production in which 'Time appeared not as an old gentleman with a scythe and hour-glass, but as Chronos, father of Zeus, and delivered his lines "seated on the globe as its ruler".'[8]

This splendid re-creation of Time hardly set the pattern for the twentieth century. Granville Barker was able to assign the part to a single actor, Herbert Hewetson, in his epochal Savoy production of 1914. The striking photograph of Hewetson is reproduced in Bartholomeusz. More often, Time must have been a casual double. Mullin's register of Stratford-upon-Avon reveals that no 'Time' was identified until 1921, when Ronald Simpson doubled Cleomenes and Time.[9] Almost predictably, Dion took the double ten years later. (Mullin, 1182.) In 1942 Archidamus was the doubling twin. Even some later productions do not list Time: it is manifestly not seen as an important part, and the last six productions listed in Mullin make no reference to Time. Whether this indicates a casual doubling, or that the part was cut, I cannot say.

It is certain though that Time was played in 1960, when 'Derek Godfrey as Time with his hour-glass struck a vein of dazzling French elegance.'[10] 1960 begins the era of the RSC, and thereafter the Company took in the interesting possibilities of Time. Trevor Nunn's production of 1969 made Time half of a conceptual double:

> Time (Alton Kumalo) was to speak the speech in its entirety in velvety black African tones in Act IV when he

appeared in the rectangular mirrored box; and Hermione's
statue, stone no more, stepped out of it in Act V. The box
became a glittering symbol, reflecting light, linking the
anguished Leontes, Time's prisoner, and the cold statue.
As in 1969 during the Dionysian dance at the centre of the
pastoral scene in which all the energies of spring seem to
burst forth in the dance of the twelve satyrs, 'the green
man' was the most exhilarating of the dancers; one could
not tell the dancer from the dance, until the green mask,
shifted slightly by the supremely natural, soaring energies of the dancing, revealed the dark face of Time.[11]

Time and the Green Man (dancer) is a double of major
conceptual weight. According to Nunn, 'As rehearsals de-
veloped, Alton maintained that his two parts in the play
were actually one part, and his largely spontaneous dance
was a re-expression of the Time chorus.'[12] Time itself
doubles as an old man with a scythe and hour-glass, and as
a young virile dancer. The casting brings out the dance
motif, which is so strong in the play's imagery, and links it
with time. It is an impressive instance of theatrical practice
fertilized by academic reflection.

Less satisfactory was the double mounted in Stratford-
upon-Avon in 1976 by John Barton and Trevor Nunn, when
John Nettles played Time and the bear:

John Nettles, who doubled as Time, did not play the bear
realistically. Wearing the formal robes of Time and carry-
ing a large, abstract, formal bear-mask, he approached
Antigonus who was down stage facing the audience. He
held the mask in one hand before his face and in his other
hand carried a stick with which he tapped the stage once,
commandingly, before taking Antigonus off. When he
came on later as Time the bear-mask was lowered, revealing a high-cheek-boned, Mongolian face.[13]

This strikes me as a rather academic conceit, since normally the double could never show in the bear. We have no idea who inhabits the bearskin. Richard David, too, found the double 'too portentous.'[14] Still, the production picked up an element in the play's design: the bear is a 'punctuating' device, as is Time. The bear signifies the Tragedy of Antigonus, which yields immediately to the onset of the larger comedy. The clearing of lungs which the bear induces in the audience is a sign that we move to a new mode, that Time renews the action.[15]

The casting of chorus has some provocative illustrations in Marlowe's work. The figure named as 'Chorus' in both the A-text and B-text versions of *Doctor Faustus* comes on as Prologue, has several speeches in the course of the play, and gives the summing up 'Cut is the branch that might have grown full straight.' The casting of this figure might seem an open question, governed only by the need to have the lines spoken with grave nobility. The A-text (1604) contains however a major clue: the speech beginning 'Learned Faustus, /To know the secrets of astronomy,' is assigned to Wagner, following the stage direction *Enter* WAGNER *solus*.[16] At the speech's end comes *Exit* WAGNER. In the B-text (1616), an expanded version of the same speech is assigned to Chorus. The easy inference is that the actor playing Wagner spoke not only the 'Learned Faustus' lines, but all the choric speeches, in early productions at least. And this is the view of the recent A-text editors.[17]

The exact nature of the A-text is still a matter of controversy, but it is generally agreed to be memorially reconstructed from the London performance. Greg's judgment, that the A-text 'appears to be a version prepared for the less critical and exigent audiences of provincial towns',[18] during the plague years of 1592–94, seems very plausible. In that case, the authenticity of the A-text includes the sanction of theatrical practice; and the scholarly standing of 'bad' quartos (however defined) has much risen of recent years, precisely because of what we can learn from them of Elizabethan theatrical practice. I take it, then, that the roles of Wagner and Chorus were doubled or combined in early productions; and this fact reflects either Marlowe's intentions or the company's sense of what was feasible and proper.

That is early practice. The case for the Wagner/Chorus double is strong in theory, too. The world of *Doctor Faustus* is the world of academe, a fact that scholarly commentary has been oddly reluctant to emphasize. The play begins and ends in the University of Wittenberg, and its central figure is a type of academic, well known to the media today, whose self-confidence encroaches upon arrogance and then hubris. The world of academe, which Marlowe knew intimately after six or seven years at Cambridge, is sketched in with some telling strokes. Consider this cameo:

> *First Scholar*   Nay then, I fear he is fallen into that damned art, for which they two are infamous throughout the world.
>
> *Second Scholar* Were he a stranger, and not allied to me, yet should I grieve for him. But come, let us go and inform the Rector, and see if he by his grave counsel can reclaim him.
> (A-text: Ormerod and Wortham, 231–36)

These two nameless academics, understudies to Rosencrantz and Guildenstern, go off to sneak on Faustus. They would; that is what informers are for. The Rector does nothing; that is what Rectors are for. Instead, he allows the situation to ripen, always a policy of mature wisdom. In permitting Faustus twenty-four years' leave of absence from Wittenberg, the Rector can scarcely be charged with precipitate action in a delicate matter. How different from Marlowe's own absence in Rheims, when the Privy Council was brought in to warn off the Cambridge authorities from clumsy and inappropriate action! But the Cambridge/Wittenberg world is clearly enough evoked at various moments in the play. That world is concentrated into its choric spokesman, Wagner.

All this bears upon the conclusion of *Doctor Faustus*, when Chorus formally seals the play. Chorus has appeared at the beginning 'in his traditional long black velvet cloak';[19] and this combines neatly with the B-text's conclusion,

> And all the students, cloth'd in mourning black,
> Shall wait upon his heavy funeral.[20]

Wagner, the man in black, would be the chief mourner. Chorus steps forward to assume his duties as leader of the rites. So the final voice, spoken by Wagner, is not that of independent moral authority, pronouncing the verdict on the fall of Faustus. It is that of timid orthodoxy, with Wagner set to inherit the tenured vacancy created by the death of his illustrious supervisor. The University of Wittenberg looks due for a period of consolidation following the abrupt departure of its most prestigious scholar; and the reactionary figure now in power warns the audience not to attempt any more escapades of the sort that got Faustus into trouble. There is both orthodoxy and irony lodged in Chorus' final words, and the rest of the play is modulated thereby.

One would like to point to a modern instance of the Wagner/Chorus double, but I know of none. Practice has been various. William Poel cast Chorus as a woman in his 1896 production at St George's Hall,[21] but no comment on the playing style survives. We are better served with commentary on recent productions, but it must be said that the productions have not been up to the commentaries. John Barton's RSC *Doctor Faustus* (1974) played obscure games with the choric casting. Robert Cushman reports that Barton 'employs the play's diabolic trinity – Lucifer, Beelzebub and Mephistophilis – to speak the Chorus of the original text; in their mouths its traditional exhortations and moralizings sound decidedly wry. The intention may have been only to provide an ironic *frisson*; but if taken seriously it suggests that the whole moral system which Faustus transgresses is diabolically controlled.'[22] Cushman appears to be controlling his disbelief; John Barber allows the adverb to indicate his feelings in 'The epilogue, adjuring us in the audience to obey Christian law, is taken from Chorus and given, astonishingly, to Lucifer himself.'[23] And Benedict Nightingale, never one to mask his perception of imperial nakedness, adds that Lucifer 'inexplicably doubles as the pious, moralizing Chorus.'[24] It would seem that Barton's idea of a world diabolically controlled found few takers among the reviewers.

The RSC is an institution that has evolved certain house doctrines over the years. One suspects an RSC block concerning *Doctor Faustus*, for Barry Kyle's production (1989) was no happier than Barton's. Here the Chorus was collective, comprising mediaeval scholars, good/bad angels, deadly sins, and demons. The transparent device of assigning a line to an actor as part of a round attempted to conceal that no one actor was capable of speaking a paragraph. The multiple chorus here came over as a make-work project for actors, a studio exercise elevated above its station. 'You might ask what the Good Angel is doing in the company of damned souls,' said Irving Wardle, very reasonably.[25] His own answer was that the entire piece was filled with a sense of dread. As Kate Kellaway saw it, 'Hell begins the moment Faustus signs the contract with Lucifer. He finds himself at a sort of nightmarish all-male pyjama party.'[26] The ordinary playgoer might well agree that it must be hell to be surrounded by men in red pyjama bottoms, all writhing on the floor; but the theological thrust is unclear. The reviewers preferred to avert their gaze from the production's most embarrassing moment, when Mephistophilis made his first entrance clad only in a loin-cloth and looking remarkably like Christ, no doubt on the grounds that Christ suffered too. As for the play's conclusion, the set of *Doctor Faustus* (at the Swan) was dominated by a high curving metal ladder, which Faustus ascended only once, at the end, so that he might descend immediately in a Hyatt-type elevator to the infernal regions. In the old days, Faustus used to be pulled into a glowing, sizzling hell. Now he simply presses 'basement.' And on this climax *Mephistopilis* spoke 'Faustus is gone: regard his hellish fall,' omitting, as well he might, the following lines in which the wise are exhorted only to wonder at unlawful things. The effect of all this was to drain the play of theological content and substitute a mere visceral sense of Faustus's fall ('how awful!'). It is clear that the RSC does not know how to cast Chorus, because it does not know how to believe in what Chorus says.

And yet the RSC, which has failed notably with *Doctor Faustus*, succeeded admirably with the choric challenge of *The Jew of Malta*. No theology is needed for the perception that Machiavelli, the Prologue, is the unacknowledged mentor of the Governor of Malta; and Barry Kyle, in his Swan production (1987) assigned Prologue and Governor as a double casting. John Carlisle, who is invariably the best verse-speaker in the Company, thus became the 'soul' of the play. He projected a finely-spoken Prologue, identical in costume and manner with the scheming Governor of Malta, the play's ultimate winner. The Governor, in Marlowe's design, is matched against Barabbas; and one reviewer noted that 'John Carlisle's pronunciation of Mach*evil* contrasts with Barabbas' disdainful mouthing of the word "Christian".'[27] The end was therefore the triumph of Machiavelli, the senior disciple outwitting the inferior one. This *Jew of Malta* had the snap of a well-oiled lock, a demonstration that Chorus may have a clear identity that yields itself to correct casting.

———

Chorus presents in sharp focus the main issues of doubling. The choric twin is either casual/inert – in which a tinge of 'virtuoso' can be taken for granted – or conceptual. If conceptual, the director undertakes to reveal the play's inner meaning, which becomes the 'super-objective' (in Simon Callow's term) of the production. Chorus cannot bear the weight of the super-objective on his own, save in *Henry V* and *Pericles*. He needs a twin to establish his identity. So the correct casting of the choric sibling is the supreme demonstration of the director's art. It is the incontrovertible proof of insight into the position, the winning move that gains the *prix de beauté*.

4

Casting the Crowd:
Coriolanus in Performance

*Enter a company of mutinous Citizens, with staves, clubs, and
other weapons.*

This is the opening stage direction for *Coriolanus*. It is a
formidable and threatening gesture, an impulse of stage
energy that is raw violence. In the play's dialectic of force
and thought, the Roman people against Coriolanus, the
people enter first. They appear and are spoken of as a collective. What does this collective mean, and how is it cast?

Terms first. It is fatally easy to slip into some such approximation as 'mob.' Commentators have often used 'mob,'
either as a general disparagement of the people, or as a
specific reference to the lynching mob in *Julius Caesar* and
hence, by ready analogy, to the populace in *Coriolanus*.
Neither sense will do. The first usage is merely a trick of
rhetoric. In the second, analogy does not work: *Julius Caesar*
is not *Coriolanus*, and the Roman people in *Coriolanus* are
disposed to debate, not rampage. 'Mob' is in any case not a
Shakespearean word. It is best to turn to Shakespeare's own
formulations.

The stage directions in *Coriolanus*, which are considered
to be authentically Shakespeare's, identify the Roman
people in varying ways. *Company*, in the first stage direction, is at least neutral, if not positive. But *Enter a rabble of
Plebeians with the Aediles* (3.1.179) is pejorative, while *Enter a
Troope of Citizens* (4.6.130) seems more respectful. At other
times we have a simple plural, *Enter Citizens*. The speech-
headings *All, All Ple., Omnes* are also used, terms that are

41

not however synonyms. *Plebeian* is a precise statement of social class and political affiliation: that is the sense Brutus fixes in 'Fast foe to th' plebeii' (2.2.185). Its associated meanings have come to be regarded as pejorative. *Citizen* has loftier claims, all of whose associated meanings are positive. A citizen is a member of a community, one whose rights and duties go well beyond a narrow allegiance to class. Since *City* is a key word in *Coriolanus* – it is used 39 times – *Citizen* has great resonance. Taking together the collective terms for the Roman people, one finds varying inflections, which encompass the respectful, the neutral, and the dismissive. If the Roman people were a single character, one would say that its identity has no single or absolute register.

Rabble focuses the issue nicely. It occurs twice in stage directions: *Enter a rabble of Plebeians with the Aediles* (3.1.179) and *Enter Brutus and Sicinius with the rabble againe* (3.1.262). What is fascinating is that *rabble* occurs twice more in the spoken text, and on both occasions the fatal word is spoken by Coriolanus, referring with his customary contempt to the people (1.1.218: 3.1.136). The stage direction, Shakespeare's, takes over the vocabulary and attitude of Coriolanus. Thus the playwright's markings of the score are something other than a reflection of cool objectivity. They are rather an index to the play's inner tensions. Are we dealing with a *rabble* or a *company*?

Then again, the matter changes according to the circumstances. The Roman people are theatrically available, and visible, only in public and in numbers. Their behavior changes according to whether they retain a sense of individuality, or form a collective in which the individual consciousness is submerged; and this sense of alternative structuring is always present. The stage direction that opens the play looks like revolt (*Mutinous*), the people on the march; but 1st Citizen's words call an immediate halt, 'Before we proceed any further, hear me speak.' After that the scene becomes a debate, not an insurrection. 1st Citizen is evidently of the militant tendency, but knows that he has to carry his fellows with him. 2nd Citizen is the archetypal working-class Tory, by no means inclined to move against a patrician with a distinguished war record. The braking element supplied by 2nd Citizen holds up the action until Menenius arrives, and he is altogether too shrewd a hand to let the tensions build further. All the impetus of the declarative stage direction is now lost; the crowd is composed of individuals, who differ, and who talk.

Much the same is true of the 'election' scene (2.3). The opening stage direction is *Enter seven or eight Citizens*. That is a large number for Shakespeare to specify, given the limited resources of his company.[1] Once again, 1st Citizen tries to raise the consciousness of his fellows, and again the mechanics of the process defeat him, for 'We are not to stay all together, but to come by him where he stands, by ones, by twos and by threes' (2.3.42–44). It is a kind of deferential canvassing, in which the people visit the candidate, not the other way round. In the event Coriolanus behaves with what is even for him extreme gracelessness, but the effect of the small groups is to lower temperatures and to permit Coriolanus, just, to get away with it for the moment.

The larger unit, the multitude, is the instrument of confrontation and denial. To this end Brutus and Sicinius work, and the Citizens take the point:

3 *Cit.*   He's not confirm'd, we may deny him yet.
2 *Cit.*   And will deny him.
          I'll have five hundred voices of that sound.
1 *Cit.*   I twice five hundred, and their friends to piece
          'em.

                           (2.3.210–213)

Not until Act 3 is the populace triumphant, and even then there are many reservations written in. Coriolanus is the most co-operative of victims, twice losing his temper (3.1, 3.3) when all he has to do is to preserve a modicum of self-control. The people have to be carefully coached by their leaders, Brutus and Sicinius, into even a semblance of disciplined unity. At other times, their main characteristic seems to be merely disorganization. That is what *rabble* implies, as much as contempt: the Roman people lack the military virtue of cohesiveness. The core of 3.1 is less a rebellion than a scuffle, marked by confusion and cross-purposes. Menenius has 'On both sides, more respect' (3.1.180) and *they all bustle about Coriolanus* (183).

Bustle (that favourite word of Richard of Gloucester) puts it neatly. These are merely people milling around, ready enough to be told what to do ('Let's hear our Tribune. Peace!') and no match for the patricians when the disparity in numbers is not too great. The stage direction *In this Mutinie, the Tribunes, the Aediles, and the People are beat in* (3.1.227) says it all. So much for democracy on the march.

I conclude, then, that the Roman crowd, as presented in *Coriolanus*, is not the fearsome manifestation of the popular will that it might at first appear. There is nothing here like the brutal capriciousness of Cade's mob in *2 Henry VI*, or the blood-lust that Antony arouses during the Forum scene. On the contrary, we see a collective of indeterminate and variable characteristics, that needs an extremely good case (handed to it by Coriolanus, most professionally worked up by the Tribunes) before it can impose its will. In the theatre, the Roman crowd poses a problem. What features will the director emphasize? The crowd's recent power, or its limitations? The crowd may excite in the audience visceral sensations of fear or delight, anticipations of the coming triumph of the proletariat associated with whatever other emotions the no doubt largely bourgeois audience may share. But the Roman crowd does not deliver on its promises, and the play ends on the effective suicide of Coriolanus, abroad. The Roman polity is undisturbed and indeed is stronger for the extrusion of its most controversial political figure. The stage has a difficult problem to handle.

———————

The first and recurring difficulty is number. It was and is hard to put a crowd on stage. Shakespeare's stage could never have seen more than a token crowd, and economics has driven us to a similar position today. There was how-ever a period of theatrical time when a large crowd was perfectly feasible. This was mainly an affair of the nine-teenth century, owing everything to that era's taste for spec-tacle and the small unit costs of the crowd. The classic production was Kemble's, which between 1789 and 1817 gave him his most famous role, together with an oppor-tunity for a numbers-based spectacle:

> In the second scene of the second act of *Coriolanus*, after the victory of the battle of Corioli, an ovation in honour of the victor was introduced with great and imposing effect by John Kemble. On reference to the stage directions of my father's interleaved copy, I find that no fewer than 240 persons marched in stately procession across the stage. In addition to the recognized dramatis personae (thirty-five in number), there were vestals, and lictors with their fasces, and soldiers with the spolia opima, and sword-bearers, and standard-bearers, and cup-bearers, and sen-ators, and silver eagle-bearers with the S.P.Q.R. upon them, and trumpeters, and drummers, and priests, and dancing-girls, etc., etc.[2]

This ovation (in which Mrs Siddons as Volumnia showed to great effect) was the primary justification for the large num-bers, rather than any political point which might be made.[3] Macready (1838) fixed upon the political dimension of the populace, doing so with evident respect and a sense of the post-Reform Bill politics of England:

> When the stage becomes animated with a seemingly countless mob of barbarians, armed with staves, mattocks, hatchets, pickaxes, and their wrongs, we become sensible that it is not a mere coward crowd before us, but the onward and increasing wave . . . of men who have spied their way to equal franchises, and are determined to fight their way to the goal. There is no mistaking the struggle for power that has begun. It is not noble against serf, but against freeman. The illusion is still further maintained by their dress. They are no longer the mere *tunicatus popellus*, who have hitherto caricatured the Roman commonalty. In many there is an approximation to the toga; and the squalor . . . is altogether done away with . . . Rome is there rough-hewn, and her sons breathe her own rude majesty.[4]

Director's theatre, is it not? And the *John Bull* reviewer had taken the point. It led nowhere though in the medium-term development of the play. After Phelps's production of 1860, *Coriolanus* had no major revival on the London stage until 1901, when Benson and Irving each produced it in rapid succession. Irving, in the twilight of his career, put it on at the Lyceum with modest success. He had no interest in raising up a revolutionary storm on his stage, and banked the political fires:

> The significance of the 'political' plot was also reduced. The Lyceum mob was neither an idealized proletariat nor a debased rabble: they were costumed as honest tradesmen, and were not very tumultuous until aroused by Marcius' contempt. Some observers found them sympathetic, and all agreed that Irving grouped and individualized his fifty supernumeraries as never before.[5]

By Edwardian standards, this was a pocket-battleship of a crowd. Certainly it was handled well, and the *Times* reviewer liked it:

> And what a crowd it is! As everyone knows, the crowd is a protagonist in this play, and everything depends upon the power of the stage-management to give it life, individuality, diversity. That power is certainly not lacking at the Lyceum. Whether the crowd is hooting or acclaiming Coriolanus, listening open-mouthed to its Tribunes, or arguing fatuously with itself, we are made to feel that it is a genuine mob and no mere pack of 'supernumeraries.'[6]

But 'fifty supernumeraries' does not seem vastly impressive, if one reflects that the crowd standard of the day was fixed by Beerbohm Tree. For Tree, the best way of staging a crowd was to put a crowd on stage. And this he did regularly between 1898 and 1913. The many revivals of *Julius Caesar* at Her Majesty's Theatre (His Majesty's, from 1901 on) presented a Roman crowd of a hundred, which was always regarded as the star of the show. We can see what it looked like from the photograph in Hesketh Pearson's biography of Beerbohm Tree. The highly disciplined crowd was a theatrical highlight of the era, above all in the Coronation Gala of 1911 when a special performance before George V and Queen Mary raised the crowd number to 250. That was and remains the largest Roman crowd ever seen on the English stage. No modern *Coriolanus* has ever had the crowd that Tree assembled for *Julius Caesar*.

Let us think of Kemble's and Tree's as the 'maximalist' position on crowds. The 'minimalist' position is, naturally, enforced by costs and the unionization of the acting corps; and in the twentieth century it has been the staple of managements. Other considerations converge. Does one really need a vast assembly? Only, surely, if a part-objective is to make the audience's flesh creep with visions of the class war fought to a finish. But this objective does not really make sense in the social conditions of the twentieth century, certainly not in England. If there was ever a 'prerevolutionary' year, it was 1919, when social disturbances in Western Europe paralleled the revolutionary wars of Eastern Europe. It is no accident, as a Marxist might say, that during 1919 there was no London production of *Coriolanus*. Indeed, J. P. Wearing, in his catalogue of the London stage, lists only one production between 1915 and 1924, an undistinguished six-performance affair at the Old Vic. The Citizens, for whom the bread discipline of Lilian Baylis was more terrible than that of Coriolanus, numbered seven.[7]

Waiting for the director is a submerged reef. If, in reasonably stable and prosperous times, one plays up the threat of the crowd, it will appear unreal. If the times are disturbed, the menace is altogether too provocative. Why not yield to the insistences of economics, and concentrate on the title role while offering a token, scaled-down crowd?

That has been the general post-second world war approach in England. Audiences can expect to see a crowd of six or seven, whose discussion in 1.1 is a straw poll of political leanings among the C1 and C2 voters. Whatever qualities this discussion may have, it can scarcely terrify the audience. It is open, naturally, to the audience to find what political moral it will. A. P. Rossiter quotes an approving review from the *Daily Worker* (parent to today's *Morning Star*) which found the 1952 production at Stratford-upon-Avon ideologically quite acceptable.[8] Even so, the post-war tendency has been to couple a small crowd with a production that is ideologically neutral, or mildly sympathetic to the people.

Coriolanus, said Kenneth Tynan, is 'a play that is best served when either everything is slanted or nothing.'[9] Perhaps so: but the record does not wholly bear Tynan out, for the only major production in this era that was heavily slanted was a disaster. In 1971 the National Theatre imported two disciples of Brecht from the Berliner Ensemble, Manfred Wekwerth and Joachim Tenschert, to direct *Coriolanus* at the Old Vic. The aim was an authentic, Marxist interpretation of the work: Shakespeare's text was to be used, but Brechtian methods applied to its production. Christopher Plummer, the Coriolanus, did not care for this prospect and withdrew at an early stage of the rehearsals.[10] He was replaced by Anthony Hopkins. The programme named seven actors as Citizens (numbered from First Citizen to Seventh Citizen) but also listed nineteen actors as 'Soldiers, Citizens, etc.' A fairsized crowd, then, by modern standards; and Robert Cushman found that 'They [the Citizens] are a formidable force, but they are not a power, for they let themselves be used.'[11] Technically, this *Coriolanus* had its virtues, but its hard Brechtian line did not make many friends and the production was soon withdrawn. Evidently, the market in England does not bear a heavily ideological *Coriolanus.*

I believe this to be a principle of production. Directors either know it intuitively, or – since 1971 – have known it from the record. Hence the minimalist-neutral approach makes a great deal of sense. In 1967, for example, John Barton's RSC production (with Ian Richardson's Coriolanus) avoided open politics. 'There is no ideological division between the masses and the nobility; all in one sense or another are equally engaged in the fight for territory.'[12] The same company, in Trevor Nunn's production of 1972, did however lavish more attention on the small crowd:

> We are in the public place of Rome, a teeming work-centre hung with a framework of stinking, blackened leather and cloth, strung with ropes and peopled not with the usual faceless extras but with individuals, carpenters, butchers, masons, crippled beggars and so on . . .[13]

This insistence on the humanity of the small crowd went with an acceptance of the Tribunes as reasonable politicians. Hence the approach, felt the same reviewer, 'is a broadly political one.' But 'broadly' is a heavy qualification and it needs looking into.

As it happens, we have some useful evidence from the next RSC *Coriolanus*, directed by Terry Hands. This was generally accepted as a totally non-slanted production, which owed everything to a stellar performance by Alan Howard in the title role and some high-quality ensemble playing. One reviewer found that 'There is no repository of sympathy in the production,'[14] thus fixing its essentially detached character. That judgment was tested in the RSC's tour of Europe in 1979, that followed the Stratford/London runs of 1977–79. David Daniell, who toured with the company, prepared a questionnaire for the audience in order to assess the audience response. One question asked whether the play as seen was thought politically to favor the Left or the Right.[15] The reactions following performances in Paris, Vienna, Hamburg, and Munich are described by Daniell.[16] A very substantial number of the respondents were unhappy with the question, and many felt that it could not catch the complexities of the play. Of those who came down, with some hesitation, on one side or the other, a majority found that *Coriolanus* favoured the Right. But this number could not have been a large proportion of the total. In all, Hands's production – whether staged in England, or on tour in Europe, a variation which in theory might make a vast difference – would seem to bear out Tynan's contention, that the play works extremely well if unslanted.

Though there is no necessary logical connection, the ideological neutrality seems at ease with a small crowd. Hands put seven Citizens on stage.[17] Whether a somewhat larger crowd is feasible was tested by Brian Bedford in his production at Stratford, Ontario (1981). The Festival Stage at Stratford is an extremely masculine, thrust stage of the

Elizabethan-adaptation type. It can accommodate some 2200 spectators, and calls for robust, even flamboyant production methods. It is emphatically not for chamber Shakespeare. Bedford – who originally wanted a much larger number – put a crowd of two dozen on stage, and deployed them imaginatively. The play opened in darkness, with a rhythmic panting sound, then light disclosed a frieze of citizens on the upper stage. The continuing presence of the people, above all in the later stages, enforced a sense of the body to which Coriolanus was ultimately responsible, and to which he answered. In the manner of that final reckoning lay the meaning of Bedford's *Coriolanus.*

This production realized a stage truth, which may not emerge from a reading of the text: the Volscian crowd that destroys Coriolanus will almost always be composed of the same actors who form the Roman crowd. It is a collective double. If certain easily identifiable actors are placed to the fore, the audience will take the point. And this is what Bedford did. In the final scene, the Roman crowd metamorphosed into the Volscian crowd. Together, under the speech-heading which the Folio designates as *All the People,* they cried 'Tear him to pieces,' and as Coriolanus pitched from the upper stage into the crowd, they fell on him and rent him. And then the Volscian people, heirs to the Romans, turned out towards the audience with looks of candid, open-eyed complicity. They had devoured the hero, and the audience became a part of that eating.

The most ambitious modern attempt to come to terms with the numbers and dynamics of the Roman crowd has been Peter Hall's production at the National Theatre (1984). And by general consent, the production failed in precisely this area. For the Coriolanus (Ian McKellen), reviewers had nothing but praise. But the crowd registered a new and controversial idea. Hall brought on to the Olivier Stage (an Elizabethan adaptation not dissimilar to the Festival Stage in Stratford, Ontario) some 90-odd Citizens, of whom ten were professional actors and the others ordinary paying members of the public. They were dressed in their normal garb, and the aim was to propose an analogue between the Roman people and the contemporary British public. That must be a key testing of the play: either the analogue is there, or it isn't. In the event, the composition of the Brito-Roman crowd gave the reviewers a chance to exercise their wit at the expense of Hall's extras:

> Shakespeare's wild, shiftless, poverty-stricken rabble didn't seem to me ideally represented by a young lady with a Gucci handbag, a beaming professorial type in tweed, a dapper City gent and several others I could mention. Nor did their sheepish meanderings, half-hearted handclappings and forlorn bleatings for Coriolanus's banishment compare very impressively with the behavior of some of their counterparts in the play's stage history: the 200-strong mob described by Henry Morley 150 years ago, for instance, which 'fluctuated to and fro, as their violent assent or dissent impelled them, with a loud and overwhelming suddenness and one-minded ponderosity, truly fearful to think of encountering.' Myself, I've seen more suddenness and ponderosity in the throng at a bring-and-buy sale than at the National last Saturday.[18]

Benedict Nightingale's sense of the historic dimension has evidently told against Hall's experiment. But he puts his finger on two genuine and unmaskable weaknesses in the concept. First, the middle-class British and tourists do not look like starving proletarians, nor are they. Second, the crowd has not been rehearsed and cannot be disciplined into a formidable machine. It is utterly dependent on the actor-leaders for a few gentle cues. Other reviewers confirm the sense of embarrassing inadequacy which the crowd conveyed. Here is Francis King:

> Peter Hall's production of *Coriolanus* suffers from one dire miscalculation. As a gesture of economy, similar to that of a rich woman who asks her guests to put their glasses in the dishwasher to save her staff work, he calls on some members of the audience, ranged in seats on either side of the stage, from time to time to get to their feet and take part as his plebeians. Elderly men then either gaze owlishly at whoever is haranguing them, or smirk in embarrassment at the audience. As we all know from the example of Mrs Thatcher, no crisis can separate a woman from her handbag, with the result that, during all the clamor for corn, a number of Mary Whitehouse clones can be seen with handbags dangling from them. The spectacle – as of a demonstration in a Home Counties village against a proposed motorway – has a certain charm. But it is also bizarre.[19]

It is possible that Hall was making a point through the very docility of the people. If so, Michael Ratcliffe, who registered the point, found it unacceptable:

> From time to time they are encouraged by the actors to shuffle forward and listen more intently to what is going on. Then they shuffle back to their seats. This is a very dumb idea since they never for a second look more than patrons of the National Theatre doing the backstage tour. Was the intention to say that the people were so wet, so indifferent, so dim?[20]

This crowd could never be an emblem of the people on the march. What, then, was the political content of the production? Michael Billington, in a generally admiring review, saw in it some coded references to the government of the day, Mrs Thatcher's Conservative administration. The crowd, for him, was entirely acceptable. They

> underline Hall's message. The brute power of a Coriolanus leads to autocracy. But popular demagogues are equally proud, vengeful and manipulative. Good government finally depends on compromise . . . This production connects directly with modern Britain to sow conviction government and popular anarchy in headlong, nightmarish collision. The stage becomes a reflection of life.[21]

That is a liberal's reaction to 'conviction' politics. It might well be an interpretation that Hall would personally endorse. Other reviewers did not see it that way. And it does seem a mild moral.

We can, I think, detect in Hall's Tribunes the dilution of this play's theatrical and political juices. Just how Hyde Parkish are the power-brokers of the people? How close are they to contemporary figures? Here, surely, is the chance for the director to make his point unequivocally. But the reviewers had little to say about the Tribunes and recorded diverse impressions. One reviewer heard a member of the audience being reminded of Harold Wilson.[22] Another saw in the two Tribunes Eric Heffer and Tony Benn.[23] Yet another perceived 'Leftist Greater London Council consulars with a Belgrano-like sourness about Coriolanus's victories.'[24]

Nobody made what seems to me the obvious point: when the production opened (December 1984) there was only one political event in England worth alluding to, the long-running Miners' Strike. It had to be the touchstone of the director's intentions, or nerve. Either a Tribune was to remind the audience of Mr Arthur Scargill, or not. And if not, the director ducked the issue.

It may be true, as Couve de Murville used to say, that 'The important things are always left implicit.' It may also be true that direct topicalities imply a vulgarity of allusion, shunned by the leading English directors. Even so, political theatre – or a production which wishes to be on terms with political theatre – cannot afford to be too muted and under-stated in its gestures. In a play of such hard, defined, and confrontational issues, one expects from the director a clear lead or a clear refusal.

I conclude, then, that the essential underlying feature of the modern *Coriolanus* in England is its disengagement from politics. From time to time, directors do indeed sketch in a political allusion. They can hardly do otherwise. But these allusions are fleeting, gestural, lacking force and com-mitment. Directors prefer to give the title-role actor his head, and to match him with a defined but small-scale crowd. I suspect that they look back on Olivier's Coriolanus (Stratford-upon-Avon, 1959) as the ideal formula for the role. 'There was a bizarre impression,' wrote Laurence Kitchin, 'of one man lynching a crowd.'[25] If the crowd looks like lynching Coriolanus, something has gone wrong with the casting.[26]

5

Casting Hamlet: Two Traditions

Casting Hamlet is a supreme challenge to the stage, and it gets no easier. In part it is simply gladiatorial, a challenge for the ambitious young actor to seek and overcome. But there is always the deeper question of the archetype, the underground identity of the part. As a way of coding the difficulties of the problem, I propose two archetypes of contemporary Hamlets, the Prince and the Rebel. One cannot pretend to bind all human complexities into one of two straitjackets. Even so, the archetypes grow out of the necessities of the text, and I think that Hamlets of the recent generation can be aligned with one or other of the great choices.

Hamlet is a prince, as the play's subtitle tells us at once. Nobody calls him 'princely,' but Horatio's final tribute is to 'sweet prince.' It is evident, most clearly in the preliminaries to the fencing match, that Hamlet has a debonair, stylish social authority, one that ultimately derives from Castiglione's *Il Cortegiano*. For the actor, an insidious question is never far away: what does a prince look like? All our contemporary models suggest a considered disclaimer: princes are not supposed to be overly princely. No Habsburg swagger, by request. Besides, the fatal charge of 'stereotype' lies in wait. 'Prince' has to be muted somewhat, and may consist of a sophisticated manner suggesting social origins within the aristocrat/gentleman band. Contrary to a prevailing impression, there has not been a dearth of princely Hamlets in the last couple of decades. A reasonable list, in no special order, would include Michael Pennington,

Daniel Day-Lewis, Derek Jacobi, Alan Howard, Edward Fox, the late Ian Charleson, and his replacement, Jeremy Northam. Of these Hamlets, Derek Jacobi's (Prospect Theatre, 1977: later BBC-TV), for instance, was decidedly Castiglionean. Alan Howard (RSC, 1970) has always found it easy to project an aristocratic presence. Michael Pennington's Hamlet (RSC, 1981) was gentlemanly and cultivated, the flower of Wittenberg University (and its drama society). So was Daniel Day-Lewis's (National Theatre, 1989). This mode is not to be played in too heightened a style, however, and Edward Fox's patrician Hamlet (Young Vic, 1982), admittedly in a weak production, was not widely admired. 'I can't think of a contemporary actor whose manner and expression are so resolutely *un*-contemporary as his. He makes Claudius seem an arriviste as well as a usurper.'[1] All of these Hamlets justified Ophelia's perception of him as 'Th' expectancy and rose of the fair state, / The glass of fashion and the mould of form.' (3.1.155–56)

The ultimate test of a prince is that he belongs as king. Olivier never seemed other than a king manqué, and this was the major criticism levelled at his film. When he turned director, Olivier transmitted something of the same approach to Peter O'Toole (National Theatre, 1963). 'More a conventional hero than a raging, destructive rebel without a cause, O'Toole's Hamlet resembled Olivier's own in its revelation of straightforward, full-blooded authoritative princeliness.'[2] As one would expect, Kenneth Branagh's Hamlet, directed by Derek Jacobi (Renaissance Theatre Company, 1988), followed in this line, and offered an Olivier-style, physical and direct Hamlet.[3] Not so different was Albert Finney's robust Hamlet at the National Theatre (directed by Peter Hall, 1975), in which Bernard Crick found 'a quite straightforward Fortinbras.'[4] The gibe lays down an important marker for the role. If Hamlet is too commanding and assertive, one will ask: how on earth did he get into this mess?

'Prince,' then, combines two strains. In style, it suggests a social ease and authority, a command of linguistic variation and sense of social nuance. In essence, it proposes a man born to be king, whom events have deflected from his natural destiny. 'Prince,' with appropriate casting, reaches out to deserve Fortinbras's final tribute, 'For he was likely, had he been put on, /To have proved most royal.'

But that is a sketch for a funeral oration. In such matters, as Dr Johnson observed of lapidary inscriptions, 'a man is not upon oath'; and Fortinbras has not met Hamlet, at least not lately. Besides, Fortinbras has his own political reasons for crying up Hamlet, whose 'dying voice' – as he wished Fortinbras to know, 'So tell him' – was for the Norwegian prince. The audience is entitled, if it wishes, to register some scepticism at Fortinbras's tribute. I turn now to the tradition of Hamlet casting that bears out this scepticism.

'Rebel' is the word that covers most of the archetype. A short list of rebel Hamlets would include Jonathan Pryce, Nicol Williamson, Anton Lesser, Mark Rylance, and perhaps the young Richard Burton (who, of course, could have claimed princely status as of right). And what does a rebel look like? Quite often, contemporary practice holds, he looks like a student. The word *student* first enters the tradition, if I mistake not, with David Warner's Hamlet for the RSC (1965). The term can scarcely be much older. Before the 1960s, people who went to university were undergraduates, not students. And in the past, Hamlets were usually too old even notionally to present themselves as undergraduates. (Irving? Forbes-Robertson? Ernest Milton?) No, our first student prince was the 24-year-old David Warner. And he demonstrated his studenthood, demeanour aside, by his garb. Stanley Wells describes him thus:

> It was obvious that this would be no princely romantic embodiment of the role. Mr Warner was, frankly, a gangling, spotty young man with traces of a Midlands accent. . . . His costume and physical appearance seemed

clearly designed not just to evoke the student at Wittenberg, but to link him with the modern student. For some of his scenes he wore a student-type gown, and a long, red scarf which seemed strikingly modern in these surroundings.[5]

This was costuming in the Elizabethan tradition of occupation-insignia. (Though Warner discarded the scarf in the London revival of 1966.) But 'student', in those pre-1968 days, connoted something different from the later stereotype. Peter Hall, the director, explained that 'in 1965 one thought that the young were very very misunderstood by their elders. We thought them beautiful, tolerant, quiet. They were flower children whose very generosity at times seemed to be apathy. One couldn't get them to react to very much. . . . there *is* apathy in Hamlet – he feels that the older generation betrayed him.'[6] Student activists came later. The concept crystallized in a moment that John Russell Brown caught: 'When pursued by Rosencrantz and Guildenstern and the officers, his "Here *they* come" is illuminated with a contemporary inflection that marks "they" as a composite description of restrictive and uncomprehending authority. . . .'[7] It was against this authority that Warner's student stood as the type of rebel. Hence John A. Mills' account of the role is persuasive:

> In Warner's reading, Hamlet became an outsider, an existential rebel, unable to accept the improvised, jerry-built value system hypocritically promoted by the adult world he was suddenly asked to enter, and equally unable to find his way to a credible alternative.[8]

Warner did not, however, yield up all the social qualities of the princely tradition; and Robert Speaight found in him 'an Etonian.'[9] The locus classicus of the rebel tradition came with Nicol Williamson's Tyneside student, in revolt at least in part against the genteel Southern Establishment. This was a notable Hamlet (directed by Tony Richardson), staged at the Roundhouse in 1969 and filmed shortly after. Irving Wardle caught a characteristic moment based on inflection: '"Who *would* fardels bear?" snarls Mr Williamson, and it is a real question, the product of a derisive, rancorous intelligence that looks at the human masquerade of crime and vanity and reduces it to a smoking heap of rubble.'[10] But John A. Mills saw that 'Williamson's accent betokened a dispossession of a deeper sort; it was the external sign, a counterpart in sound, of an alienation that was not social but existential.'[11] This Hamlet lived with a dispossession that far preceded Claudius's usurpation. And one could never say of Nicol Williamson that he was likely to have proved most royal. He was always *The Bofors Gun* maverick handing out trouble to the authorities, without having any taste or capacity for it himself.

The startling power and intensity of Williamson's Hamlet injected into the rebel tradition a quality that has never, I think, altogether left the part. It is latent, waiting to be revived. On this line of approach, Hamlet is not a dispossessed insider; he is a natural outsider, notwithstanding his birth. Hence the rebel/outsider formation has an inner logic and cohesiveness. I offer a few characteristic illustrations. Robert Lindsay, at the Barbican Roof (directed by Braham Murray, 1984) was 'scruffy. . . . looks like a motor mechanic.'[12] Another reviewer saw him as 'very much the student; a volatile L.S.E. rebel very much in tune with his times and his audience.'[13] 'Student', we can note, has become virtually a term of abuse. In a world where we are forbidden so many avenues of abuse, it is convenient to have 'student' as available and sanctioned. Anton Lesser, at the Warehouse (directed by Jonathan Miller, 1982) seemed 'more at home at a polytechnic than Wittenberg University'.[14] (Lesser was the Hamlet who cheated Laertes in the fencing match: one feels that polytechnic students are getting a bad name through their association with Hamlet.) Then again, Mark Rylance's neurotic Hamlet for the RSC (directed by Ron Daniels, 1989), who spent much time lolling, pyjama-clad, on his bed, looked to one reviewer 'like the kind of student who hangs around the canteen at Essex University.'[15] It is no part of my brief to prefer charges against LSE, Essex University, and polytechnics; but when Hamlet recalls to a reviewer a student from these institutions, the actor does seem to stand in dock charged with a nameless offence.

Still, a rebel does not have to be a student. Another, older concept re-emerged in Peter Stormare's Hamlet for Ingmar Bergman's production (the Royal Swedish Theatre, which came to the National Theatre in 1987). This Hamlet was a notably charmless neurotic, even a psychopath,[16] well observed by Sheridan Morley: 'Hamlet himself is played largely in sunglasses and a black raincoat by Peter Stormare, who seems to be what they have in Stockholm instead of James Dean.'[17] The reference is to *Rebel Without a Cause*. Is that a fair statement of Hamlet's position?

It has, of course, been long accepted that there is something in Hamlet which goes beyond the facts of the case as stated. There is always something unaccounted for in Hamlet. Yet 'rebel' makes deep if necessarily imprecise claims. At bottom it may be address to the world, *'Je suis contre.'* This is existential gesture: or, at a higher level of consciousness, Jimmy Porter's claim that 'There aren't any more good, brave causes left.' On the same theme, and coming from the same era, the 1950s, *Rebel Without a Cause* is a Romantically self-confirming claim ('No cause is up to my high standards'). The claim does not, I think, attract too many admirers today. One tends to ask, against what is Hamlet supposed to be rebelling?

In the first place, Claudius. I suppose the marker is Basil Sydney's sly, rather bloat king in Olivier's film. But this is not at all par for the course today. Michael Billington makes a commanding, and surely sound generalization: 'In most recent productions (with the exception of John Barton's) it has been blindingly obvious that Claudius is the only fit person to rule Denmark.'[18] True, and one often sees an actor of distinction, in the prime of his career, making a first-class case for Claudius. Thus Alec Clunes, whose account of a man suffering for his *crime passionnel* held its own against Paul Scofield's second Hamlet (1956); thus Denis Quilley, more authoritative than Albert Finney's Hamlet (National Theatre, 1975); thus David Waller against Alan Howard (1970). One could list many more. Such actors are simply not going to be played off the stage by Hamlet, and they make moreover a powerful if implied plea to the audience perception. It may be that Abraham Sofaer pointed the way, even in Gielgud's last Hamlet (Haymarket, 1944): as Kenneth Tynan saw it, he 'managed to capture an altogether remarkable slice of audience sympathy, and so restored the balance of a play too often obscured by the eclipsing charm of its hero.'[19] I don't doubt that Tynan put his finger on the effect of Sofaer's playing, but 'eclipsing charm' will ring a little oddly in the ears of today's playgoers. As I guess, the general audience perception has in time shifted from 'Poor Hamlet: what a hard time he is having' to 'Look, somebody has to run the country, and Claudius is making the best of a difficult job.' Claudius has always been a strong part, but today it embeds itself in a context which is subtly supportive of him, and as subtly sceptical of Hamlet.

I suggest, then, that we are not simply looking at a line of strong, contemporary Claudiuses. One expects to see Claudius well and sympathetically played, certainly, just as one is surprised to see a buffoon Polonius. Standards have risen markedly in the playing of the middle-upper middle range of parts. But there is more to it than that. Audience sympathy, which as Tynan indicates used to be largely at Hamlet's disposal, is now more evenly distributed between Hamlet and Claudius. There is a case for Claudius, Polonius et al.: they make it. They are the Establishment, they are other people. And is the Establishment so hopelessly corrupt, after all? At the National Theatre *Hamlet* which Richard Eyre directed in 1989, Jeremy Northam made even Osric an intelligent and supple courtier, one who understandably sees Hamlet as a threat to the realm which must at all costs be neutralized. Perhaps we have a better general understanding of the problems of government nowadays. So the case for Hamlet is more rigorously assessed.

'Student' is not, of itself, going to crash any ontological barricades. An actor who too closely resembles a student will soon reach the limits of his appeal to the audience-counsellor. What, one wonders, is he complaining about? Student loans? Family bereavement? Sexual problems? The world of *A Very Peculiar Practice* is not one in which cosmic tragedy is enacted. As for 'rebel', rebels need a cause. The stage needs to know what a really repressive régime looks like, so that it can simulate one. The Eastern Europeans have been most helpful, but this vein, culminating in the Romanian *Hamlet* that came to the National Theatre in 1990, seems at least for the present to be worked out. If the stage is driven to a Third World dictatorship for its *mise-en-scène*, this is an open admission of the real problem: that Hamlet (as traditionally proposed) does not fit too well into our own society. If then we call him a 'misfit', we have defined him, terminally. The network of assumptions that sustained the older, Romantic Hamlet starts to collapse as soon as one examines them. The anti-Romantic Hamlet may stem from the actor's perception that the Romantic case will not do. Jimmy Porter played better in 1956 than today.

Then again, even the part of Hamlet is under pressure, or rather responsive to the gravitational pull of *King Lear*. A generation ago most people, if asked, would have said that *Hamlet* was Shakespeare's greatest achievement. They would have found the question slightly odd, since the answer was very widely accepted. Today, a large proportion – a majority of academics, as I guess – would vote for *King Lear*. With its coverage of age, declining authority, collapsed and pluralist world view coupled with open-access casting, it seems to hit a contemporary nerve. For the actor, the casting point is crucial. There are still some restrictions on the casting of Hamlet. Anyone can play Lear, or hope to; it is the great option for mature actors. If Noël Coward were revising *Present Laughter* today, he would consider changing Gary Essendine's Peer Gynt (the part he yearned for) to King Lear. Hamlet is the part an actor never had. Lear beckons.

Hamlet, then, remains a vacancy ready to be filled, 'a series of lines to which an infinite series of claimants arrives and competes for.'[20] Jonathan Miller's view of the latest candidate as 'the Tichborne claimant' suggests that all are imposters. In a sense, they all are. But they have a particular problem today, princes and rebels alike: their claims are easy to file and hard to prove. Some vital nutrient, on which Hamlets feed, is missing in contemporary society. When it returns, we shall know it unmistakably, because Hamlet will tell us so.

6

Lear's System and Cordelia's Aside: Leading the Audience

'In his sane moments Lear hardly ever makes an intelligent remark.'[1] Trenchant as always, Orwell directs us to the key issue of the play's opening, and therefore of the play. He cannot be taken too literally. Intelligence does not always express itself in manifestly 'intelligent' observation. Still, if Orwell is essentially right, the opening ceremonial is a mere dotage. And this is a view commanding wide support. 'In the first scene of the play, Lear is a foolish old man . . . who is led in the vanity of dotage to stage a scene to gratify his craving for affection.'[2] Thus Kenneth Muir, in the New Ardon. For Wilson Knight, 'A tremendous soul is, as it were, incongruously geared to a puerile intellect.'[3] These are solidifications of Bradley's perception of the event:

> The rashness of his division of the kingdom troubles us, and we cannot but see with concern that its motive is mainly selfish. The absurdity of the pretence of making the division depend on protestations of love from his daughters, his complete blindness to the hypocrisy which is patent to us at a glance, his piteous delight in these protestations, the openness of his expressions of preference for his youngest daughter – all make us smile, but all pain us.[4]

Bradley had obviously been unlucky with the productions he saw. Accept his perception, and a dimension of the tragedy is already irrecoverable. *King Lear*, on the view cited, shows us an old fool who, tautologously, commits an act of folly, thus confirming the soundness of judgment of those who have written him off as an old fool. To be taken in by Goneril and Regan, whose hypocrisy is patent to us! Not a commentator in the land would be deceived by them. Such a man deserves our pity, not our sympathy. King Lear is already being ushered, gently, towards the geriatric ward. He will not be accorded there the dignity of intelligent choice, of responsibility for his actions. But his energetic ravings will be followed closely, and his death allowed as cathartic.

Now Bradley's position is not, of course, universally accepted. The opening ceremonial has its purpose, like all ceremonials. Elder Olson puts it well: 'if Lear is giving up his authority and still wants security and dignity, he can only trust to their love; and his insistence upon their public profession of it is an attempt to have it warranted and witnessed as a formal part of the compact of the delivery of property and power.'[5] The public affirmation of love is an exercise that no power in the world disregards. In the same vein, Winifred Nowottny writes that 'At the heart of Lear's tragedy there lies the great problem of traditional symbolic forms. These are the only language of love and reverence; they have, however, to be maintained against attack, and the function of authority is to enforce reverence of form on those who repudiate it.'[6] That is pertinent and true; but Nowottny goes on to say that 'Authority takes the tragic step of asking for a token of love beyond that reverence for the forms of duty it knows itself able to enforce, whilst at the same time abrogating its powers.' That, I think, is more questionable. Asking for a token of love, clearly, is neither unreasonable nor wrong. And Lear, with reason, believes himself to be capable of enforcing it. It is the form of Lear's question that irritates ('Which of you shall we say doth love us most'), by its pretence that extent and quality of reward can be made immediately commensurate with the love-protestation. That is a logical absurdity; but it is the form which Lear imposes. In any case, the language of formal protestation is often hyperbolic to the point of absurdity. When the Spaniard says 'My house is yours,' he merely means that one is welcome. The form of words that Lear chooses to cue in the love-protestation is not, in itself, a cause for rebellion or proof of dotage.

The Olson-Nowottny line does narrow the 'folly' of Lear's early actions, since it cedes to him the dignity of staging a ceremonial that is valuable and pointed. But such writers defend only the ceremonial itself. They have little or nothing to say concerning the substantive arrangements that Lear has in mind, which are generally thought of as indefensible. I propose here to consider the political hinterland of the opening scene, the dispositions which Lear makes for the security of his realm.

———

King Lear is a tragedy of identity, in the sense that the King has created a system that is his own identity. It is precisely a play of old age, for its subject is responsible for arteriosclerotic structures of rule that malfunction through their rigidity. Nevertheless, the failure lies in that rigidity, not in the structures themselves. Lear's system of rule is perfectly logical and has seen him safely into his eightieth year.

The system is based on competition and rivalry among Lear's dependents. With three children-dependents, that is an easy game to play, but its dynamics are complex. Goneril has presumably married first, but has no children, and her full dowry has yet to be determined at the play's opening ('With my two daughters' dow'rs digest the third,' 1.1.128). Regan likewise has married, has borne no children, and awaits her dowry. Cordelia is destined for a Continental alliance, but it has not yet happened, and her child-bearing potential is yet to be tested. Everything is open-ended, undetermined, requiring the King's will to co-operate with events as they occur. And the King wishes it that way. France and Burgundy, 'Great *rivals* in our youngest daughter's love,' have been frozen in that posture of rivalry: 'Long in our court have made their amorous sojourn' (ll. 46–47). Their position is figured in the opening scene, for France and Burgundy have to wait offstage for matters to be concluded onstage. The negotiations have been stretched out to the limits. Only at the last moment will the King decide.

Uncertainty in the governed is the secret of government. Lear keeps everyone guessing. The point about the opening lines is not only that the division of the kingdom is fixed, but that Kent and Gloucester (who are better placed than anyone else, elderly and privileged courtiers near to the King) are taken by surprise. *Kent*: 'I thought the King had more affected the Duke of Albany than Cornwall.' *Gloucester*: 'It did always seem so to us . . .' Only in his opening speech does Lear 'express our darker purpose.' And even here, the small print is worth looking at. His opening gesture is maliciously unsettling: 'Our son of Cornwall, / And you our no less loving son of Albany' (ll. 41–42) is a reverse bid, for the later precedence (Goneril, Regan) would seem to call for Albany, then Cornwall. (Cornwall must think, for a moment, Have I got it? Albany, Have I lost it? The thoughts of their ladies must run interestingly parallel, but not geometrically so.) And then, the dowries. 'To thine and Albany's issue' (l. 66) is at once ambivalent, sceptical, reserved. If one reads it 'To [thine and Albany's] issue,' there's no problem. If there's a fractional pause after 'thine,' it comes out as 'To [thine] [and Albany's] issue.' The old man is saying: 'If you can't bear Albany a child, he may have to look elsewhere. If Albany can't give you a child, *you* may have to look elsewhere. If you want future trouble, try to arrange the succes-

sion for someone who isn't "thine and Albany's issue".'
Without taking the banal pro-Goneril position, one does see
her point of view.

Regan gets terms that are similar, if not identical: 'To thee
and thine hereditary ever' (l. 79). This is clear enough, surely?
Not to me. To begin with, there's no mention of Cornwall,
so Regan has theoretically more room for manoeuvre than
Goneril, whose issue is coupled with Albany's. Then much
depends on the Folio's comma after 'thee.' All modern editors abandon that comma, and most of them leave the line
open to inflection and parsing. Two consequences flow. If
we retain the comma, it means that the territory is be-
queathed to Regan; and thereafter to her heirs. 'Hereditary'
thus becomes a noun, for which there is no instance cited by
the *OED*, but that of course is no conclusive argument against
Shakespeare's creating a noun for the occasion. If we abandon the Folio comma, we understand, if we do not insert, a
comma after 'To thee and thine.' That makes 'hereditary' an
adjective, as it is in the seven other instances in Shakespeare. But it leaves 'thine' open (thine and Cornwall's, or
thine alone?). The salient point is that 'hereditary' is not
'issues': heirs are not the same as children. There is no need
to look beyond the *OED*'s first sense of *hereditary*: '*Law and
Hist*. Descending by inheritance from generation to generation; that has or may be transmitted according to definite
rules of descent; legally vesting, upon the death of the holder,
in the person designated by the law as his heir.' One can
effortlessly imagine the lawyers having good sport, as
Gloucester would put it, over the terms of Lear's will. What
it means for the moment is that Regan has secured a better
deal than Goneril. She has much wider terms in which to
dispose of her inheritance; she has greater freedom from her
husband; her power to dispose is power to propose, simply
power. And she has earned it.

Regan has earned her reward by surpassing Goneril. Her
prize-winning speech is quite different in quality from her

sister's. Peter Brook recounts a telling anecdote, of how he asked an audience member (to whom the play was unfamiliar) at a lecture to read Goneril's first speech. She did so, 'and the speech itself emerged full of eloquence and charm. I then explained that it was supposed to be the speech of a wicked woman, and suggested her reading every word for hypocrisy. She tried to do so, and the audience saw what a hard unnatural wrestling with the simple music of the words was involved when she sought to act to a definition . . . [Goneril's] words are those of a lady of style and breeding accustomed to expressing herself in public, someone with ease and social aplomb. As for clues to her character, only the façade is presented and this, we see, is elegant and attractive.'[7] In other words, Goneril is trying – successfully – to reconcile the needs of a public occasion with her own sense of identity. Regan is evidently another matter. Her speech is indefensibly glutinous and false in tone. But this merely ministers to Lear's requirement, and he demonstrates that the winning competitor receives the rewards of competition: which include not only the territory (fixed, in advance) but the terms on which the dowry is made over (open, until Lear speaks). It must be dispiriting to be asked by Lear to bat first. The other side always has a target, and should score more heavily.

Goneril and Regan are rivals, not close allies. Obviously, the course of the play bears this out. I need to stress the point here, because Shakespeare artfully contrives a different impression at the close of the first scene. The intimate, prose-after-verse dialogue, political in tone and context, leads to an easy misjudgment. It conduces to a perception of legend: here are the two Ugly Sisters, ganging up on poor Cinderella as they always have. I point out that the dialogue can as easily be read the other way. Goneril and Regan are *not* close; the opening address, 'Sister,' is cool and functional, and no first-name terms are exchanged, nor is the 'thou' form. Anyone who has ever quoted 'Let us hit together' will know that one addresses the remark not to friends, but to (temporary) political allies of whom one needs to be wary. Why should Goneril say it now, if she and Regan have been practising the injunction already? Cordelia, so far from being Cinderella, is her father's favourite daughter, set to receive her father's greatest gift: Prince Charming, and the best third of the kingdom. Let us examine the elements of Lear's gift.

It is an error of interpretation to go all the way down the Stonehenge route. *King Lear*'s primitivism is not in doubt, yet at least two distinguished productions of recent years (Trevor Nunn's for the RSC, 1976, and Robin Phillips', for Stratford, Ontario, 1979–80) have set the play successfully in the nineteenth and early twentieth centuries.[8] We perceive in the play civilization and its discontents, not merely a falling-out of Druids. Similarly, the play's locations and titles are far from lost in the swirling mists of pre-history. There are five British place-names in *King Lear*: Albany, Cornwall, Gloucester, Kent, Dover. They are hieroglyphs of value, from which a complete system can be reconstructed. The map that Lear calls for its real.

'Albany' signifies Scotland, or the northern region of the Island. The Variorum quotes Holinshed:

> The first and last part of the Island he allotted unto Albanacte hys youngest sonne . . . This later parcel at the first, toke the name of Albanactus, who called it Albania. But now a small portion onely of the Region (being under the regiment of a Duke) reteyneth the sayd denomination, the reast beyng called Scotlande, of certayne Scottes that came over from Ireland to inhabite in those quarters. It is devided from Loegres also by the Humber, so that Albania as Brute left it, conteyned all the north part of the

Island that is to be found beyond the aforesayd streame,
unto the point of Cathenesse.[9]

'Cornwall' is the western region, together with a portion of
the heartland. 'Gloucester' fits easily into the system, for the
Earl of Gloucester is the Duke of Cornwall's vassal: this
approximates to our sense of Gloucestershire as being, rather
tenuously, connected with the West Country. Always one
must think of titles as denoting possession of land, and not
as empty honorifics. There is no name for Cordelia's portion, but it must be the South-East jut of the Island, together
with its share of the heartland. That, indeed, would bear out
Lear's statement that Cordelia is to 'draw/A third, more
opulent than your sisters' (ll. 85–86). Kent's regard for
Cordelia is more than a purely personal sympathy. She
would have been his regional overlord. Dover is the regional port.

Through Dover, the Continental alliance is activated.
Which alliance is it to be? Bradley puzzled over this: 'Why
Burgundy rather than France should have first choice of
Cordelia's hand is a question we cannot help asking, but
there is no hint of an answer.'[10] In his footnote he speculates
that 'Burgundy is to be her husband, and that is why, when
Lear has cast her off, he offers her to Burgundy first.' I doubt
this. At the point when Lear offers Cordelia to Burgundy,
all bets are off; the explosion has already occurred. If we
read any significance into the order of asking, my earlier
point applies: to speak first, in Lear's system, is to accept the
position of disadvantage. But the French alliance is manifestly preferable. The Duchy of Burgundy was always
land-locked (save, apparently, for a brief spell in the tenth
century when there was a claimed opening to the Mediter-
ranean). No easy, maritime communications could exist between Burgundy and England. France offers an inexpugnable
base, with the eternal assurance of support for or intervention in British affairs, just as in the subsequent play. It

would always have been France, in the competition for
Cordelia's hand. Burgundy was there to make it an auction.

But should not Lear have preserved the Unity of the
Kingdom? That is the sort of second-rate maxim that a first-
class fact rebuts. If the kingdom is to be united, it must be
under Albany. Albany, a man who spends most of the play
backing off from his responsibilities, and in the final page
offers, incredibly, to abdicate *twice*! (Once to Lear, once to
Edgar and Kent.) To abdicate in favor of an abdicator is
scarcely the pinnacle of political wisdom. And Albany has
no children. Since Britain was not actually united under a
Scots king until 1603, one wonders at those who reproach
Lear for not arranging this coup, one thousand years ahead
of its time. We need not be concerned with the questions an
appointments committee might raise concerning the moral
standing of Cornwall. It is sufficient to note that he has
married the second daughter, has no children, and operates
from a base in the South-West, from which at no time in
history has the Island ever been governed. The political
problem is not which of these unappealing satraps to hand
over power to. It is to set up a system which will survive
Lear, while permitting him a guiding hand in late old age.

That system will not be a unitary state. Rather, it will
illustrate, and indeed dramatize, Lear's propensity to di-
vide and rule. The post-abdication outcome will be a dy-
namic tripartition, which is the political extension and
reflection of Lear's relations with his daughters (and sons-
in-law). Put differently: in what sense *is* the Britain of the
play's opening a unitary state? It is already divided, as it
must be, into regional suzerainty, with a quantum of bad
feeling thrown in ('future strife,' predicated on the under-
standable attitudes of the three daughters to each other).[11]
What maintains unitary rule, of a sort, is precisely the policy
of sectional division which Lear has successfully pursued.

We now have the essence of Lear's gift to Cordelia. She is
to receive the most desirable portion of Britain, the South-

East, together with a Continental alliance, probably France. To call these dispositions 'favouritism,'[12] as though the term were self-refuting, is to miss the point. ('Favouritism,' said Admiral Fisher, 'is the secret of efficiency.') Cordelia holds all the cards. By continuing Lear's balancing act, she can dominate Goneril/Albany and Regan/Cornwall, playing off one against the other. Even if they combine against her (inherently unlikely, on personal grounds), an established realm of the South-East, with Continental backing, should easily hold its own. If Cordelia should bear a child, that opens up the prospect of a future reunification of the Island under her issue. Over these agreeable political manoeuvres the elder statesman will preside, happy to continue the great political game while monopolizing ('We two *alone*') his favorite daughter. I see no folly in this scheme. On the contrary, it appears to me that Lear has planned his retirement rather well.

All Cordelia has to do is to accept the gift gracefully. 'At a moment where terrible issues join, Fate makes on her the one demand which she is unable to meet,' says Bradley. 'Cordelia cannot, because she is Cordelia.'[13] Most people, I suppose, go through life under the impression that Fate is imposing a series of unfair demands on them, which by sheer ill-chance they are unable to meet, because they are themselves. To have this impression sanctioned by Bradley goes some way towards accounting for Cordelia's popularity – and perhaps Bradley's. It is unnecessary here to sift the range of emotions and motives which Cordelia may be supposed to experience. (Though I would add to the traditional range Cordelia's sense of being placed in a false position, that the combination of suitor-choice and dowry-division ought not to be synchronized with a declaration of filial love.) She mutinies, anyway. Lear, predictably and with justice, is wounded and shocked. Has he not done everything a King and father can do to ensure the stability of the realm, and the security and happiness of his favorite daughter? Does he not merely ask to be given a vote of thanks, for the record?

More, has not Cordelia committed the grossest of solecisms? The opening scene is a great public spectacle, the division of the realm. It is theatre of monarchy. On such occasions the roles are determined, the individual compressed within the part. For the individual to assert self against the programming is, in this context, intolerable. It is like using an award-giving ceremony to make a radical speech, an action widely despised. The general understanding is plain: if you don't like the ceremony, stay away; if you come, you enter into a compact to abide by the rules of the occasion. There are decencies which in aggregate conduce to the decorum of existence. Cordelia, in making her demonstration, flouts them all.

Are these reflections available during scene one? Not at all. Shakespeare stills such thoughts as subversive to his immediate dramatic purpose. He does so with the simplest of technical tricks, the aside. When the actress swivels round, eyes the audience directly, and asks 'What shall Cordelia speak? Love, and be silent,' there is no question of an option. We have been got at. The audience is bidden, not invited, to take Cordelia's part. It is tampering with the jury, but no one ever said that drama should be fair. Nothing in this explains the tragedy. It merely explains our immediate responses. Thinking comes later. With it, we can recognize that the aside is a form of ingratiation that no other character in this scene is permitted to practise. Lear, above all, has no aside. This is a case that Shakespeare has no intention of allowing his immediate client to lose.

Suppose those two devastating appeals to the jury were struck out, what then? It has been done. Peter Brook, in his RSC production of 1962, was widely and erroneously criticized for cutting the post-blinding Servants' dialogue;[14] but he retained Cordelia's asides. He also cast the glamorous and appealing Diana Rigg as Cordelia, allowing her as the traditional focus of audience sympathy. But when Brook made his ensuing film of *King Lear* (1969), his thought had moved to an even bleaker statement of the play. The film Cordelia was an abbreviated part, by no means attractive or engaging; and her asides were cut. The film audience was given no reason to side with Cordelia, or indeed with Lear. On the contrary, the case for Goneril – the outrageous behaviour of the knights, Lear's impossible entourage – was fully rehearsed. Neither early nor late was there an easy resting-point for the audience. (Kozintsev's film, also of 1969, offered a traditional, radiant Cordelia, complete with aside.) Brook's later version of *King Lear* may appear as a branch line in theatre history. It remains a powerful questioning of the natural flow of the play, a text as we receive it that is determined to support Cordelia. Cordelia/audience becomes a special relationship, which the more impressionable of commentators take over, eventually translating their esteem for Cordelia into the honorific 'Christ figure.'

Bradley's transports over Cordelia ('She is a thing enskyed and sainted'[15]) are well known, but still astonish. Dover Wilson temperately describes her as 'conceived as a Christ-like figure.'[16] As Jonson remarked of Donne's 'Anniversary,' 'if it had been written of the Virgin Mary, it had been something.' But this is no place to indulge in a critical brawl over whether Christ-figures ought so readily to precipitate tragedies in Act 1 through suppressing their Christ-like qualities of humility and compassion. I shall confine my remarks to the technical. Cordelia's part is defined by its brevity, both in length and in style. She is indeed laconic, even if her reputation for saying little is grounded upon talking out of turn to the audience. The part is easy, verging upon the actress-proof. And it is a part that does not show signs of extensive re-writing between Quarto and Folio. Shakespeare had no important second thoughts about Cordelia. He did not need to.[17] Cordelia is to be retained within an intense, narrow band of effects; any expansion would create ambivalence, additional possibilities, a shade of reservation. Her role is to ambush Lear in Act 1, be reconciled with him in Act 4, and make a final appearance symbolically and actually carried by Lear. To continue the metaphor, I conceive of Shakespeare as counsel directing his client: *'And don't say another word.'* Excellent advice, and it continues to dominate *Lear* criticism.

The catastrophe occurs because everyone is fixed in a role which is rigidly maintained by the programming of State. The daughters' functions are prescribed. Cordelia, in rebelling, brings upon herself the unappeasable wrath of the State's main agent. Kent, 'Tis my occupation to be plain' (2.2.93), is blunt when any second-rate supple courtier could and should avert the crisis by calling for an adjournment. By confronting Lear, by losing his temper ('Be Kent unmannerly/When Lear is mad. What wouldst thou do, old man?' [ll. 145–46]), Kent offers his master no escape, and compels him to *be* King. Everyone else keeps clear, beyond staying Lear's hand from homicide. Lear himself sees the reimposition of monarchic rule as the only response to the provocation:

> Hear me, recreant, on thine allegiance, hear me!
> That thou hast sought to make us break our vows,
> Which we durst never yet, and with strain'd pride
> To come betwixt our sentence and our power,
> Which nor our nature nor our place can bear . . .

> (ll. 168–72)

In the theatre of State, all works perfectly so long as everyone hews to the role. A single rebellion and the system is fractured; no one knows how to repair it. In the scene as written, it takes only three hotheads and a crowd of innocent bystanders to make a catastrophe.

The impressions we receive, and are meant to receive, of the catastrophe are subtly at odds with the judgments we arrive at later. Lear commits an irreparable folly in banishing Cordelia, but his appraisal of forces, up to that point, is highly defensible. Goneril and Regan have a case, whatever their later conduct. Kent's loss of temper, like Cordelia's, is unpardonable: they have a duty to handle an elderly and splenetic monarch, a duty which can hardly come as a surprise to them. The Continentals look different, too. France has evidently not seen *1 Henry VI:* if he had, he would remember that the much-derided Henry married for love, not State, a decision seen and demonstrated as disastrous. Burgundy, so apparently pusillanimous in his scene, has done well in staying clear of the British entanglement, and of Cordelia's advanced sense of duty. The realm of Burgundy, at least, will be spared the ministrations of a Christ-figure in Act 5. Nobody will remember Burgundy anyway. Even the actor has to get changed into one of the minor military functionaries, and may end up being ordered to execute Cordelia. The play, in fact, tries to put the opening scene out of mind. But this it cannot altogether succeed in doing. In the theatre we are all naive spectators; but we retain the faculty of memory; our backward glance does not confirm in all respects the impressions of the opening.

What the play has done is to evoke, in a distorted and nightmarish way, some premonitions of the opening and of Lear's mind. The French alliance becomes the French invasion. Regan's freedom to bequeath becomes the claimed right to make Edmund Earl of Gloucester, and her agent 'In my rights/By me invested' (5.3.70–71). Lear's curse on

Goneril's fertility (1.4.272–78) foreshadows the state of all three daughters. If there is one moment in the later stages that is a cracked echo of the earlier, it is Lear's glimpse of a future in which 'We two alone will sing like birds i' the' cage' (5.3.9). It is not so far from the opening, and his confession in the aftermath of shock – it is conceivable that he never told Cordelia – 'I loved her most, and thought to set my rest/On her kind nursery' (1.1.123–24).' Of the tragedy of *King Lear* there will be as many formulations as spectators. Not least, I think, of the tragedies is that the final stages mock Act 1, and Lear's not despicable, not unintelligent vision of order.

7

Laughter in *King Richard II:*
The Subplot of Mood

The best-kept critical secret of *King Richard II* is that there
are jokes in it, or at least moments when the audience is
not discouraged from laughing. One may read widely in
the commentaries without encountering this truth. In the
theatre, *King Richard II* is well known to pose problems of
laughter-control, and this is reflected in some distinguished
commentary. Sir John Gielgud confesses himself unsure as
to whether the Aumerle scenes should be retained or omit-
ted.[1] 'Certainly the rhyming couplets in these scenes have a
strong flavor of fustian melodrama, and many of the lines
can seem ridiculous unless they are delivered with consum-
mate power and tact.'[2] Sir John alludes to a stage tradition
of cutting the Aumerle scenes, which A. C. Sprague saw as
dominant.[3] In the same vein, Stanley Wells remarks of the
Aumerle scenes that 'Shakespeare is trying, not quite successfully, to achieve a subtle fusion of seriousness and comedy for which he cannot command the necessary technical
resources, so that the comedy tends to submerge the seriousness.'[4] Wells is writing a propos of John Barton's RSC
production of 1973 (the most successful *King Richard II* of
the last two decades), and tells us that the 'gage' scene was
re-written, so as to come over with no hint of comedy.[5] J. C.
Trewin, again, has several warnings on the dangers of actors overdoing things in their search for comic effects.[6] These
comments come from a vast communal reservoir of stage
experience. They constitute a traditional and powerful view
of *King Richard II*, which goes like this: the play's primary
effect is a high, stylized decorum; this effect is however

challenged by certain comic possibilities which threaten the play's tone; it is the business of directors and actors to suppress, or at least keep within very strict bounds these licensed but subversive tendencies. It is further argued that Shakespeare was not quite in command of his material here, and it is therefore legitimate for the director to bind up these 'young dangling apricocks,/Which like unruly children make their sire/Stoop with oppression of their prodigal weight . . .' (3.4.29–31) As a practical problem of theatre, I make no doubt that the comic possibilities have to be conveyed with tact and precision. But the traditional view of *King Richard II* does the script less than justice.

To my knowledge, the most penetrating academic criticism of this aspect of the play comes from Sheldon Zitner. He concludes that

> The Aumerle conspiracy scenes, then, are not necessary for the success of *Richard II* in the theatre. They may even inhibit it. They mock its elevation and seriousness; they riddle its style. They destroy the fine trajectory of emotion that ends in the intensity of Richard's murder in Pomfret Castle and the eloquent guilt of Bolingbroke in the last scene. They strike at almost everything that moves us in the tragedy. Yet they greatly enrich the play.[7]

Zitner has the right sense of paradox here: the Aumerle scenes spoil the play, yet they enrich it. But evidently, paradox is not enough as a justification for these scenes. The charges that Zitner lists are a recapitulation of neo-classic criticism of Shakespeare from the seventeenth century on: the issues never really change. I prefer the simple principle, that everything in a Shakespeare play belongs there. If Shakespeare built in certain powerful effects, then we can only begin by acknowledging their legitimacy. These effects however reach out well beyond the Aumerle conspiracy. They can I believe be detected microscopically in the earliest scenes; and their symptoms are audience laughter. One can approach the matter via the casting and playing of the major roles, and the inherent qualities of some scenes.

Richard is an ironist, and actors may choose to emphasize irony as the cutting edge of the part. We have J. C. Trewin's assurance that the night's first words, 'Old John of Gaunt, time-honoured Lancaster' are 'often ironically stressed.'[8] With that kind of entrance-note, the rest follows naturally. Alec Guinness, for example, played Richard as 'a proud weakling who employed irony as his defence.'[9] Jeremy Irons offered 'a glazed preoccupation and ironical remoteness from anything but the effect he is making at any given moment.'[10] The most thoroughgoing ironist I have seen, Brian Bedford (Richard Cottrell's production at Stratford, Ontario, 1983), used his polished irony to mock the knightly tomfoolery of 1.1 and 1.3. There are certain lines, as Bedford demonstrated, that can be treated with something less than deference. 'How high a pitch his resolution soars!' (1.1.109) invites the note of cool disdain. The line verges on the aside, as Richard invites the audience to share his view of Bolingbroke's cadenza. It is a deflating, puncturing moment, like Pucelle's rejoinder to the English herald's catalogue of the dead Talbot's titles. The same trick is worked after Mowbray's long, passionate outcry, 'A heavy sentence, my most sovereign liege' (1.3.154–73), which meets the dismissive 'It boots thee not to be compassionate.' (Bedford changed the word to 'so passionate,' a respectable stage emendation that brings out the modern sense of the line.) Again, Bedford picked his way hesitantly through 'As he is my father's – brother's – son' (1.1.117), as one who is trying to get right a tricky genealogical problem (and thus, sending up the world of heraldry). 'Our doctors say this is no month to bleed' (157) has the same resonance. In all this –

and throughout the preparation for the tournament special in 1.3, when a bored Richard exchanged jokes with his Queen – Bedford presented the King as an aesthete, fallen among noisy hearties, whose dearest wish is that these muscular braves would give over their interminable wrangling.

The Spirit Ironic, speaking through Richard, necessarily induces a number of audience laughs: not guffaws, but audible, appreciative responses to the controlled mockery in the actor's inflections. Opportunities scarcely visible to the reader's eye are there for the actor. Irons made his audience register the 'high Herford' pun (1.4.2), and his Aumerle raised a laugh at 'What said he when you parted with him?' 'Farewell.' (1.4.10–11) This is the 'What did he say?' joke that Shakespeare exploits in *Richard III*, 3.7.23–24. Then again, the scene's ending is clearly comic, as Richard II takes on the mode of Richard III. John of Gaunt's passing is analogous to Edward IV's, and Richard strikes the same chord with

> Come, gentlemen, let's all go visit him.
> Pray God we may make haste, and come too late!

> (1.4.63–64)

To which all chorus, 'Amen.' I noted enough of such moments at the Irons and Bedford performances to be sure that they were in accord with the score, and were not tokens of the actors' will to ingratiate themselves at all costs. What are the laughs *for*? They are an organized reaction to the oppressive decorum of the piece. They imply, what we might well guess, that Shakespeare does not take nearly so seriously as the participants their view of themselves. They begin to formulate that mental distaste, or even moral queasiness about the action, that anticipates the structures of the assured masterpieces of the Henriad. For a critique of the action one looks in the first place to a clown – there is none in *King Richard II* – or the 'ranking' figure, Richard himself. He is ideally placed to project superiority over, if not a critique of, the play's values and actions. Richard has at least an inkling of what is wrong with the Middle Ages: too many aristocratic hotheads, front and centre, brain-damaged by an excessive regard for chivalry.

One would have said, viewing the text, that in the first act at least the Spirit Ironic must express itself through Richard or not at all. And yet this reasonable judgment turns out not to be well founded. Barry Kyle, in his 1986 production for the RSC, cast Michael Kitchen as Bolingbroke and allowed him to give a highly individual flavor to the part. Kitchen's mannered, fastidious delivery detached Bolingbroke from the play; and Michael Billington was not alone in seeing this Bolingbroke as 'an ironic Pinteresque opportunist who by a time-slip has landed up in mediaeval England.'[11] From his entrance line, 'Many years of happy days befall/My gracious sovereign, my most loving liege!' (1.1.20–21), Bolingbroke embraces insincerity as the cardinal virtue. If there is a moment when he believes his own words, it is at

> How long a time lies in one little word!
> Four lagging winters and four wanton Springs
> End in a word: such is the breath of kings.
>
> (1.3.213–15)

and he realizes, for the first time, what it means to be a king and destroy time. Irving Wardle saw Kitchen's Bolingbroke as 'a small, ironic, and most unregal figure. He is not a flintily calculating adversary who intensifies Richard's pathos. He inhabits a world where pathos and lyricism have no place. He has urgent business to complete and, from the start, he looks on wearily while his relatives are striking rhetorical postures.'[12] That is it, exactly: Bolingbroke is the man outside rhetoric, and thus outside the play's dominant style (though he is of course able to adopt it on occasion). Without being the play's raisonneur, Bolingbroke triumphs because he understands it, is not taken in by the play's style. Here too the ironist can glean his harvest of audience appreciation, as Kitchen did. His success inclines one to a re-statement of the play: there is certainly a spirit of irony abroad, but it does not have to cast Richard as its sole or even major spokesman. The charge is looking for conductors.

Act II comes to the relief of the perplexed director, for here the Duke of York joins the breakaway movement from the play's announced style. This amiable old booby cannot move outside his character-note scene in 2.2, when he is plainly not up to it and keeps telling us so. 'I know not what to do . . . Come sister – cousin, I would say, pray pardon me . . . if I know how or which way to order these affairs, / Thus thrust disorderly into my hands, / Never believe me . . . Well, somewhat we must do . . . All is uneven, / And everything is left at six and seven.' (2.2.98–121) One quite sees that actors, viewing these lines with greedy relish, have to be shackled by directors. The strong law has to be put upon Bottom-type Yorks, otherwise they will simply pick up the production in their hands and walk home with it. But really, it is impossible to argue against York being a part of substantial comic possibilities.[13] The idea that the Duke of York is a nobleman and therefore a seemly fellow cannot live with the lines. If we need a further argument, the trigger pulled by the Servant is conclusive:

Servant   My lord, I had forgot to tell your lordship:
Today as I came by I called there –
But I shall grieve you to report the rest.

York   What is't, knave?
Servant   An hour before I came the Duchess died.

(2.2.93–97)

The audience might just be prepared to give decorousness a chance, and set its collective face into the mask suitable for a Sad Moment; but York destroys this chance with 'God for his mercy!' Unregenerate and unworthy sections of the groundlings will take this to mean 'What a bit of luck!' especially if York traitorously rolls his eyeballs at them here. This suspicion is not allayed by the long speech that follows, when York does precisely what the Servant has done: he forgets the Duchess. The Servant's memory-lapse is a trick that Shakespeare used again for a comic effect in the final stages of *Cymbeline:* 'O Gods, I left out one thing that the Queen confessed,' which is somehow funnier if the actor amends to 'O God' (retaining an inflection of Blackadder). The stage, as always, is something other than the mirror to nature. What in real life has to be suppressed ('Poor old so-and-so is totally forgetful these days') is in the theatre a shameless bid for uncivilized reactions. Memory loss is funny.

York presides, if that is not too grand a term for him, over a disorganized resistance movement to the themes of tragedy, elevation, pathos, and lyricism. In a play written entirely in verse, he is the surrogate prose element, through whom the claims of prose are filed if not administered in absentia. The final stages of Act V, of course, belong to Richard and are so ordered from the start. The larger Act IV (so often the problem act in Shakespeare) belongs to the Yorks. Let us review the main features of these indecorous passages.

The opening of Act IV, set in Westminster, offers a striking scene of noble contention set in the mode of chivalric dispute. *Enter as to the Parliament* Bolingbroke and the other great lords. It is a pageant of the era – Gothic révival, one would say – calling for stained-glass windows as part of the *mise-en-scène*. Bagot makes his challenge, and Aumerle responds with 'There is my gage, the manual seal of death, / That marks thee out for hell' (4.1.25), of which one can say that had not Shakespeare written the lines, a Wardour Street hack undoubtedly would. A moment later Fitzwater joins in with 'There is my gage, Aumerle, in gage to thee' (l. 34). By line 46 we have Percy, 'there I throw my gage.' Oppressed by the need for elegant variation, Another Lord rephrases the challenge: 'there is my honour's pawn' (l. 55). Small wonder that Aumerle, beset with gages and pawns (and according to some editors, hoods), can only stand at bay with 'Who sets me else? By heaven, I'll throw at all!' (l. 57) This ought to stem the tide but fails. Surrey, impressed by the pawn variation, joins the peer group with 'In proof whereof there is my honour's pawn' (l. 70). With the score now standing at 3–2, gages and pawns, the knightly contestants are running out not only of terms but of gloves. Fitzwater is reduced to 'There is my bond of faith, / To tie thee to my strong correction,' and kindly editors explain that he has already thrown down one glove and must part with the other. Did the gage-hurling classes go about with one gage only, maintained for the sole purpose of ceremonially challenging competitors? Aumerle it would seem belongs to this persuasion, for he is now reduced to borrowing a glove from a compassionate bystander. 'Some honest Christian trust me with a gage/That Norfolk lies – here do I throw down this . . .' (ll. 83–4) 'Trust me with a gage' implies, I suppose, that Aumerle intends to give it back afterwards. I think we have to infer a ceremonial glove, for ostentation not use, which the well-appointed nobleman habitually carried around if bent on stately quarrel.

Bolingbroke, who has now taken over Richard's position in scene one, seizes the moment to intervene with 'These differences shall all rest under gage' (l. 86), and repeats the line at

> Your differences shall all rest under gage
> Till we assign you to your days of trial.

> (4.1.105–6)

I would ask anyone doubting the import of this scene to count the gages. I make the score seven, and am ready to admit that anyone raiding the text for inflections could squeeze out one or two more gages. Is it conceivable that Shakespeare, writing in 1595 or so, was unaware that repetition is funny, inescapably so?[14] Why, then, is this scene not generally recognized as the subversive cell threatening the play's tone? Quite possibly, because nobody has ever seen it played in full. I am sure that I have never witnessed a heap of seven gages. J. C. Trewin, who must have seen as many performances as any man, does not positively state that he has witnessed seven gages: 'In my experience the house has usually begun to laugh at the third, and mirth grows slightly hysterical when one of the lords becomes a gage collector.'[15] Directors cut, and cut again, to overcome a challenge which they feel they have to resist. The question remains on the table: why fight it? Only a Pre-Raphaelite could paint the Westminster scene, and only a Pre-Raphaelite painter could take it seriously.

By Act V, scene two the murder is out. There is a gloomy consensus that boots are comic, and York, calling for his boots, resists yet again the impulses of directors to bring him within the emotional orbit of Richard. No doubt there is something intrinsically comic about boots – one thinks of Sir Wilfull Witwoud – and there is rich business in the servant helping York to don his boots, against the Duchess's

imprecations. Since York exits before the scene's end he has
either succeeded in getting his boots on, or, worse, has
departed boots in hand to complete the operation without
interference. More, we have here a marital conflict which, if
somewhat below the Strindberg-Albee level, still belongs to
the world of comedy. At 'Peace, foolish woman,' 'I will not
peace,' 'Make way, unruly woman' the audience's reactions
are commanded, not invited. But there is no case to answer
here. Everyone agrees that this scene of, as it were, boot
camp is not to be masked, only controlled. The same judgment applies to 5.3 when the Yorks plead for their errant
son. Once again the principle of repetition is invoked; and
the spectacle of York, his Duchess, and Aumerle kneeling
together is not one to harrow the soul. One's mind is irres-
istibly drawn towards Sheridan's stage direction, *exit kneeling*. It becomes a vertiginous mental prospect at the scene's
end. All this has been cued by Bolingbroke himself, 'Our
scene is alter'd from a serious thing' (5.3.77), in which the
scene's ranking figure admits regretfully that a change of
tone is forced upon him, and us. It is the play's major
variation of tone before Exton moves in.

I am reluctant to invoke a disreputable old friend, 'comic
relief,' but I fear he cannot be excluded from the discussion.
It seems clear that Shakespeare feels that the piece needs to
be saved from the oppressive decorum associated with the
tragic fall of kings, and certain passages reflect this plan
unmistakably. They are there for tonal variety. My argument is that the plan cannot be confined to the Aumerle
scenes, especially 5.2 and 5.3. I think the Westminster scene,
4.1, is much funnier than it is generally allowed to be; and
there are earlier moments when the dramatist makes it easy
for the actors to glean a legitimate laugh. Such laughs come
readily from an ironist Richard, but as we have seen an

ironist Bolingbroke is playable. And yet, there is a detectable resistance among reviewers to comic effects, and this is usually focused upon the Duke of York.

In 1951, for example, Anthony Quayle directed *Richard II* as the first of the season's cycle of histories at Stratford-upon-Avon. The *Manchester Guardian* reviewer criticized 'turning the palsied irresolution of the Duke of York into a joke as Michael Gwynne seemed set upon doing to loud laughs from an audience which might have known better.'[16] But the highly-experienced W. A. Darlington felt that Gwynne 'carries out very ably a new idea that the Duke of York is merely a figure of fun.'[17] 'New idea': if Darlington is historically accurate here, and one would expect him to be, then the comic Duke of York is a post-war development notwithstanding Poel's earlier essay. By 1964, Charles Graves could write that 'It is customary to play York's hesitation for laughs, and Paul Hardwick's interpretation was no exception to this.'[18] That was written of Peter Hall's production in the masterly RSC cycle, and Hardwick's performance evidently stopped well short of buffoonery. Often one can see a line of RSC tradition: Hall's judgment of the role's parameters must have influenced Terry Hands's RSC production of 1980. In this, Tony Church successfully knit together the part's possibilities. 'Tony Church's Duke of York, the shilly-shallying old man Richard leaves in charge of the kingdom, is a valid comic creation, rich in human detail.'[19] Note 'valid': Church o'erstepped not the modesty of nature. Critics are always on the anxious lookout for immodest Yorks. B. A. Young was happy to find that York was 'never without dignity even if he is tugging his boots from below his wife's feet.'[20] The clue here is that Church twice played a distinguished Polonius for the RSC, and has made it clear that the old statesman is something other than the cartoon that Hamlet derides. The bloodline is York: Polonius. The trick is to get the balance of qualities right.

But Yorks persist in violating decorum, and critics continue to repress them. In the RSC's 1986 production, Irving Wardle thought Bernard Horsfall's York 'a *commedia* pantaloon.'[21] Michael Coveney thought that 'The Aumerle plot against Bolingbroke . . . is played desperately for laughs before meaning.'[22] For Eric Shorter, 'Bernard Horfall's Duke of York isn't afraid of playing for laughs, though whether he ought to get as many as he does is another question.'[23] I cite these as illustrations of a reviewer's tendency, to defend the decorum against the challenges. My own view, pace Mr Coveney, is that the meaning lies in the laughs. Shakespeare is mounting a challenge to the world of *King Richard II* which is not formulated by any one member of the cast. The challenge is diffused, unlocalized, yet unmistakable in its directional force. Trewin remarks of the gage scene that 'It is odd why this should defeat an audience':[24] I should prefer to say that the audience is in no way defeated. It is registering precisely what Shakespeare wishes it to register. One has to look at *Troilus and Cressida* to see what Shakespeare was pondering in *King Richard II*, whose dramatic expression he assigned to the brush-fire laughter of the piece. The values of chivalric gesture are under fire in both plays. The laughter, covert and open, of *King Richard II* looks forward to the words of Thersites.

8

Metamorphoses of the Audience

The playhouse audience finds often a collective analogue to itself on stage. On many occasions, the stage holds merely a number of individuals, with no special characteristics. They are a plurality rather than a group. But on occasion, the stage personnel coalesce into a group with marked corporate identity. It may be a mob, a congregation, an army. In such cases the tendency is for the audience mind to be replicated on stage: that is, our involvement with the stage events leads us to become part of, or closely involved with, the army, mob, and so on. The nature of this group is thus basic to our experience of the drama. In organizing his dramatic scenarios, Shakespeare blocks out this experience with the utmost care.

One factor common to all these groups is that they are in varying degrees an 'audience,' people listening to others on stage. That is true but truistic. I do not pursue here the sense in which the stage collective is also a stage audience, as happens with all play-within-a-play scenes. The discussion therefore excludes the Mousetrap scene in *Hamlet*, the Worthies' show in *Love's Labour's Lost*, the mechanicals' play in *A Midsummer Night's Dream*, and all direct mirrors of the playhouse audience. My concern is with those stage collectives that are something other than open extensions of the watchers.

I make a leading assumption about the Elizabethan staging of these scenes. When there is a prime speaker, such as Henry in his Harfleur/Agincourt addresses, or Cade in the mob scenes, I regard him as commanding the central position, in the middle of the platform stage.[1] The soldiery or mob is lined around three sides of the stage, quite possibly facing inwards towards the speaker. Thus the speaker, in addressing his stage audience, is in the mode of direct address to the playhouse audience: we look at the speaker through, or over, the horseshoe of stage listeners. This is much easier to imagine if we now register, what was not known before 1989 and the Rose excavations, that the floor of the Rose auditorium was raked downwards towards the stage. If this was true of other theatres including the Globe, and it seems likely enough, then the playhouse audience (boxes and groundlings) had a much better angle of view than was thought, and could better take in a speaker not anchored to the front of the platform. On such occasions, the playhouse audience finds its own physical analogues lining the stage. Its own reactions, its own identity, are in part stimulated by the horseshoe of watchers. I do not press this sense of the staging, however, which in any case could not apply to all the scenes in the discussion. Staging is always a massive variable. The main objective here is to grasp this shifting identity of the stage 'audience', and relate its feelings to those of the playhouse audience.

I begin with the Council scenes in *Troilus and Cressida* (1.3 and 2.3). These scenes clearly assume the playhouse audience to be part of the *Council*, or *committee*, which is realized on stage. We are auditors, without the privilege of speaking, but our opinion matters and Agamemnon and Ulysses address us directly. We go through the usual silent agonies of the committee. (Not Nestor again, for heaven's sake. Does he always have to repeat what the Chairman has just said?) Everyone, even Ulysses, the one man with genuine brains, has to make a statement of principle before he can get to the point. How familiar it all is. Still, the public tone is even in the Greek debate. Things are more contentious with the Trojans, among whom the young Turks, appropriately, make the running. Here the Chairman fails to assert himself. The only breach of protocol however comes from outside the two councils (Cassandra), not from within. The decorum of the two scenes is that of the committee, and it shapes our reactions. Most of us have been there before.

Then, take the Harfleur and Agincourt speeches in *Henry V*. The mode is direct address to the playhouse audience, screened through the horseshoe of soldiery lining the platform. The dynamics of the Harfleur speech, which is an objective and historical failure, stem from the opening line: 'Once more unto the breach, dear friends, once more.' There has already been an offstage repulse; now the King speaks to an Army-audience that is rooted to its place. The residual Sitzfleisch of the playhouse audience means that it is disinclined to follow the King, especially as it is buttonholed by Bardolph, Nym and co. following the King's exit. We become, if you like, camp followers or at least fringe units of the Army of Normandy. It is no use the Commanding Officer haranguing us in slightly hysterical terms, the drift of which is that if one doesn't feel brave one can at least act it. We are not going to follow him into the breach today. It is not one of our more glorious episodes.

All this is changed at Agincourt, when the dynamics are reversed. Here, it becomes a heroic action for us to retain our seats. The King offers us crowns for convoy. Not a bit of it. We intend to stay where we are and see this thing through. We are going to pick up our Normandy ribbon, with the Agincourt clasp. Henry's Agincourt address is successful, as the Harfleur is not; and it is all done on an exact assessment of what the Army-audience is to do, whether to stay or to go. The corporate identity, and performance, of the audience is that of the *Army*.

Next, *crowd*. 'Crowd' is far too convenient a word for me to let it go, but the term is broad. Crowds have differing characteristics, and I offer some categories.

(a) The crowd in *Julius Caesar* is properly so called in the Forum scene (3.2). These are Citizens, numbered and clearly identifiable, who retain their individual characteristics and discuss amongst themselves Antony's points in the intervals which he leaves them. The Citizens do en masse change their minds, but they do so as the result of conscious reflection which has been worked upon with great rhetorical skill. What the Forum scene shows is a series of dramatized Gallup polls, in which the Roman views are found to be shifting. This is a crowd, but not (until the very end) any sort of mob.

Mob, however, is the only term for the same Romans in the lynching scene that follows (3.3). There are still individual speakers, but rational individual traits have departed. There is now a single mind to destroy and kill, a will that merely pauses until it finds the trigger ('Cinna') that will release its next act. Anything would have served. The mob is what the crowd has become: it is a collective abdication of individual responsibility, a refuge for those elements of the mind which it is the business of ordinary society to keep under guard. The lynching scene is the great emblem of stage violence in Shakespeare, the triumph of the subconscious will made manifest.

(b) The crowd in *Coriolanus* should not be termed a 'mob' because it does not lose its head, and is generally under the control of its leaders, the Tribunes. For me, the Roman crowd in 1.1 is best characterized as a *debating society*. They may be 'mutinous', and carry 'staves and clubs', but they are disinclined to go looking for patricians to dismember. What they really want is to talk. And this they do, in what emerges as a nineteenth century Working Men's Institute debate, with two articulate and competent speakers. They debate politics warmly but civilly, until the guest speaker arrives. Menenius, a smooth old sophist, knows too many debating society tricks for the plebeians, and is easily able to impose on them through his fable of the belly. (Just as Henry was able to baffle his own discontented troops on the eve of Agincourt, with that long and dishonest argument 'So . . .') Note that the 1st Citizen, who has no time for Menenius or his class, still accords him a fair hearing. The civilities of the debating society determine the encounter, which is by no means the raw episode of class war that it might at first appear.

(c) For what might seem a genuine mob, one turns to *Henry IV*, Part Two, and the Cade scenes. This is not however a true mob, because it is under the sway of Cade (until he loses control), and the playhouse audience reacts to Cade rather than his followers. The mechanism is detailed in 4.2. Cade's speeches to the crowd will be, like Henry and Antony in the earlier instances, direct addresses to the playhouse audience, who are ranged behind the followers of Cade. However, Cade's words are intercepted and subverted by the asides which flow between Dick and Smith. These two comment freely and libellously on Cade's ancestral pretensions. Thus, the playhouse audience is not so much in the crowd as on the fringe of the crowd – a quite different affair. (Cf. the Monty Python version of the Sermon on the Mount. 'What's that he's saying? Blessed are the *Greeks*?') Dick and Smith, with their covert anti-Cade chaff, perform a neat job of derailing Cade's announced programme and subliminally assuring the audience that all will come to nothing. The stage audience are spectators of a Hyde Park demagogue; they give him a (derisive) hearing but are not really convinced. Cade's fall is already prefigured.

And this occurs in 4.8, when the crowd obviously becomes an *electorate*. It listens to the election address of Cade (the people's candidate, with a programme based on a vast dispersal of wealth to the general public), and Buckingham and Clifford, standing in the conservative interest, who promise a general amnesty coupled with a profitable invasion of France. There will be loot for all able-bodied males. It is a winning programme and the electorate, as usual, turns away from radical adventurism to the safer ways of social gain under patrician leadership. The Cade scenes are not really a mob on the rampage, but the record of a Card pushing his luck too far; and it ends as Eatanswill. The crowd, after all, is the people, making a perfectly coherent decision as to where its interests lie.

(d) All the above instances assume that there is something innately threatening in a public assembly. But this need not be so, or at least need not be an assumption of stagecraft. Crowds can be genial and well-disciplined. Even *Julius Caesar* begins with the Roman crowd in what Rosalind would term 'a holiday humour'. Flavius's opening address.

> Hence! home, you idle creatures, get you gone!
> Is this a holiday?

must surely resonate before an Elizabethan audience, some of whom are statistically certain to be playing truant from work. Some giggles and other reactions to Flavius there, I fancy. His question, 'Is this a holiday?' is a straight invitation to the audience rudesbys to respond 'Yes!' Thereafter the seriousness of Marullus imposes itself on the jokiness of the Roman crowd: the Tribunes drain off the holiday humour. Still, the opening mood of the onstage crowd is close enough to that of the playhouse audience.

Again, the final stages of *Henry VIII* show the audience mind being absorbed into that of a good-natured crowd. The event is the birth of a royal princess, attended by the anxiety of the crowd gathered outside the Palace to see what it can of the babe. During the penultimate scene, that crowd is off-stage but a felt presence. For the last scene, the crowd materializes on stage and is the immediate conductor of the emotions transmitted between king and audience.

That crowd listens, rapt, as Cranmer makes his great prophecy on the future Queen Elizabeth, and as Henry makes his supremely tactful acknowledgement of his subjects' good wishes. The play ends on Henry's 'This little one shall make it *holiday*,' at which the stage (and doubtless playhouse) audience will break out into cheers which become applause. The onstage crowd become cheerleaders for the audience, and the happy geniality of the event unites all in the house.

In all these instances the 'crowd', that loose but indispensable term, has a changing but assessable corporate identity. I now turn to some cases where the identity of the collective is fixed, but whose relationship to the playhouse audience is indirect or exists as subliminal inference.

Jury is problematic. The arraignment of Hermione in *The Winter's Tale* and the 'trial' of Katherine in *Henry VIII* are not true trials, and do not call for consideration here, but *The Merchant of Venice* is cardinal. Everyone refers to the fourth-act climax as the 'Trial Scene', and its dramatic implications are worth pursuing. This is a case in which the presiding Judge is also the Head of State, and there is no onstage jury. There is therefore no direct analogue with English legal processes, and Shakespeare (like Jonson in *Volpone*) is careful to indicate that the Venetians do things differently. Nevertheless, while Shakespeare retains certain hints that the Venetian State has a few tricks in reserve,[2] the general impression is clearly that this is a fair hearing. The events of that scene form a narrative, emotional, rhetorical, and legal, whose outcome we do not know until the end. The appeal is to the playhouse audience in its implied role as jury. Indeed, it is easy for the Duke to bring in the general audience with a gesture: 'Shylock, the world thinks – and I think so too –' It is not difficult to envisage the Duke calling into existence a jury-audience, the 'world'. Before the 'world' Shylock argues his own case, while Antonio is represented by Portia: we are spectators at this moral and legal clash, turning now one way, now the other. The jury will feel, among other emotions, concern for Antonio, admiration for Portia, distaste for Gratiano, and at the end a certain revulsion at Shylock's defeated exit. It is a mixed verdict that the jury brings in. The modern stage finds the Duke's direct address hard to re-create; but Komisarjevsky, in his 1932 production at the Stratford proscenium, rigged up some cutouts to represent an onstage jury.[3] That great director thought it necessary to remind the Stratford audience of its role, which in the Trial scene is that of jury service.

Congregation is difficult for the dramatist to handle. Apart from the possible implications of blasphemy, the interior of a church creates too many associations for Shakespeare to feel happy inside it. His dramatic purposes are not served by direct reference to onstage congregations. This emerges fairly clearly in *The Taming of the Shrew*, where Shakespeare passes up an obvious chance to make capital out of Petruchio's outrageous conduct at the altar. In the Burton-Taylor film, the director (Zeffirelli) could not resist the temptation to make something of the altar scene; but Shakespeare, faced with the eternal choice, show or tell, chose to give Gremio the set-piece account. This strikes me as a conscious and reasoned evasion of certain dramatic difficulties, the turning of a problem into an opportunity. Much the same is true of *The Winter's Tale* (3.1) where Cleomenes and Diomedes report their visit to the Delphic Oracle. I have seen this passage staged as a direct re-creation of the Delphos temple, with fair success (Stratford, Ontario, 1986), but Shakespeare prefers to keep his religious mysteries on the level of reportage.

The difficulties cannot be evaded in *Much Ado About Nothing*, where the dramatist's design calls for a church scene (4.1). Shakespeare's handling of that scene is instructive. There is absolutely no attempt to build up (or allow to develop) the feelings normally present amongst a congregation. Indeed, the development is abrupt in the extreme. The scene opens with Leonato's 'Come, Friar Francis, be brief,' and the very next speech is the Friar's 'You come hither, my lord, to marry this lady?' Shakespeare cuts directly into his 'plain form of marriage' and does not permit the audience to re-assemble its thought as a congregation. Within moments, the scene has become an awkward and graceless denunciation, a 'scene' made by Claudio of which the general audience are fascinated and perhaps embarrassed witnesses. Thus, though the action is formally assumed to take place in a church in Messina, there is no collective formation of a 'congregation' mind. The option is refused.

These matters have to be veiled or implicit, if they exist at all. I have no doubt that they do. Ultimately, the secular church that is the theatre will convey its authority to all those present; and it can best do so at a play's end, most notably at the mysterious closures of the great tragedies. But my final candidate for the 'congregation' mind occurs in the last moments of *Love's Labour's Lost*. In the great and serious atmosphere that surrounds the news of the King's death, that unseen benign autocrat ruling over comedy, the songs of spring and of winter come as balm. Hymns to the seasons of life, they are religious in import. Then Armado comes forward. He (and not Sir Nathaniel, the play's parson) becomes the play's priest, and he speaks in the moment and accent of the benediction:

The words of Mercury are harsh after the songs of Apollo. You, that way; we, this way.

9
Dramatis Personae

The publication of the new Oxford Shakespeare[1] is a chance to assess the current state of dramatis personae listings. The obvious comparisons are with the Riverside Shakespeare, the Bevington Shakespeare, and certain recent single-text editions in the New Arden, New Cambridge, and Oxford series.[2] Not a great deal has been written about the difficulties of categorizing the dramatic identities of the actors,[3] and yet the value of the enterprise is patent.

Any attempt at a rigorous system of listing the actors breaks down at once. There are at least two major reasons. First, the Folio offers 'The names of the Actors' (or 'The names of all the actors,' or 'The Actors Names') after only seven plays. They are *The Tempest, The Two Gentlemen of Verona, Measure for Measure, The Winter's Tale, Henry IV, Part Two, Timon of Athens,* and *Othello.* All other listings derive from Rowe. An editor must therefore abandon the Folio 'Names' or seek to assimilate them into his own listings. Second, all human beings are capable of re-definition in terms of relationships. All fathers are also sons. They may also be husbands, cousins, friends, and so on; the editorial choice will often be one of convenience rather than system. There can be no clearly-marked exit from these problems. The inquiry becomes, as usual, an assessment of what is happening, and the Oxford Shakespeare is clearly the place to start.

I.   FOLLOWING THE FOLIO

Since there are no 'Names of the Actors' in the quartos, the seven Folio plays so provided are the basis for a new listing of dramatis personae. The problem, as one soon discovers, lies in the archaic quality of some of the descriptions. There is no difficulty, say, with *Alcibiades, an Athenian Captaine*, which can be transferred to a modernized text with no change other than the loss of the final 'e'. That is what editors invariably do. But no editor would dream of categorizing Falstaff, Pistol and co. as 'Irregular humorists,' were it not that the Folio enjoins him to. The Oxford solution is to retain 'irregular humorists,' though with inverted commas, by which one is to understand a quotation from the original source. This convention is not, however, spelled out; and it runs into the further difficulty, that parallel citations from the Folio are not always so identified. One can of course agree that it is pedantic to encase 'country justices' with inverted commas, since this is what Shallow and Silence unarguably are. It would look odd to acknowledge the Folio at this point. But what of other descriptions which contain at least a strong flavour of archaism? Would a modern editor propose, on his own initiative, Speed as a *clownish servant*, or Apemantus as a *churlish philosopher*? The Oxford retains these identifications, but without inverted commas, while Lucio, 'a fantastic' (with inverted commas) evidently acknowledges the Folio's *a fantastique*. Some terms which are archaic are expanded into larger descriptions, thus enabling the quotation marks to be dropped. The Folio's *Caliban, a salvage and deformed slave* becomes 'CALIBAN, a savage and deformed native of the island, Prospero's slave.' Similarly, the Folio's *Barnardine, a dissolute prisoner* becomes in the Oxford 'BARNARDINE, a dissolute condemned prisoner' (again, without inverted commas). Surely 'dissolute' is a word never used today without irony? There are always, as it were, invisible inverted commas around it, which 'present' the word. 'Virtuous' is similarly placed. Are we to understand that unidentified irony is an unacknowledged quotation? The mixture of ancient and modern, with and without open identification, sits un-easily in the Oxford. The borderline is between those de-scriptions which can passably be assimilated into modern English usage, and those which remain so outlandish as to call for a gesture of detachment. At stake is the central issue of modernization, and the extent to which the Folio's ter-minology remains a foreign body resisting assimilation into a new system.

II. MODERNIZATION

The problem is present in other dramatis personae listings, where the editor is not constrained by the Folio. Some archaisms are almost inevitably intrusive. 'VERGES, the Headborough, Dogberry's partner' contains a term that has dropped out of existence. It can scarcely be recovered. But it occurs in the stage direction (Quarto and Folio) at the begin-ning of 3.5 and cannot be passed over. A director might be tempted to see Verges as a Deputy Chief of Police, but such licentious solutions are not for the editor. 'Partner' is un-satisfactory, since the word suggests equality and Verges is subordinate to Dogberry. Is 'partner' intended as a gloss on 'headborough' or as additional information concerning Verges' relationship with Dogberry? The Oxford seems here to conflate and confuse lexical and non-lexical information. The proper solution is doubtless to let 'headborough' stand, though with an immediate footnote.[4] The *OED*'s 'petty con-stable' covers function, and indicates relationship with 'constable' well enough.

A more muted form of difficulty arises when one applies a word in its later sense to a category belonging to the past. I am not altogether happy about 'PORTIA, an heiress' (still less with the Bevington/Riverside *a rich heiress*: would one bother to speak of an heiress who was not rich?). The *OED* says that 'heiress' was introduced in the 17th century, and

gives 1659 as the first usage. I suppose we think of the term
as current in the 18th century and archetypal in the 19th
century (Henry James, say). The legal and other constraints
of Portia are not those of Washington Square. I prefer
Dover Wilson's *a lady of Belmont*.

The problems of modernizing women are always with
us. Phrynia and Timandra, in *Timon of Athens*, are a test for
the sensitive editor. The Folio offers no help here, ignoring
them in the dramatis personae. Even the stage direction in
4.3 gives only their names. Dover Wilson, Bevington, the
Riverside, and H. J. Oliver's New Arden (1963) combine to
list Phrynia and Timandra as *mistresses to Alcibiades*. The
provocative 'mistresses,' a term that has now the singular
property of being inappropriate wherever applied, is
quietly dropped by the Oxford in favour of the inoffensive
'whores.' The social ambiguity attendant upon 'mistresses'
seems unsuited to camp followers.

A clear case of an unhappy archaism is the Oxford's 'Don
Adriano de ARMADO, an affected Spanish braggart.' 'Braggart,' which is found in the text and speech-prefixes of
Love's Labour's Lost, does not belong in the dramatis personae. Richard David, in his New Arden edition (1955),
remarks in his note to 5.2.536 ('The pedant, the braggart')
that 'These are generic names of stock characters in Italian
comedy.' But in modern English, 'braggart' is misleading,
for it means one who is boastful, swaggering. This is the
reverse of Armado, with his exquisite, ultra-sensitive cour-
tesy. Hence I much prefer the solution of David, Dover
Wilson, the Riverside, and Bevington, who give *a fantastical
Spaniard*. A patently obsolete term is one thing. A misleading term is something else.

III.   SOCIAL RANK AND IDENTITY

These exercises in modernization clear the way for the bulk

of my examples, which are not directly affected by questions of obsolescence, or which present them in yet subtler ways. In essence, the challenges to a modern editor are not so different from those confronting Rowe. Who are these people? How can they be succinctly described? To what extent can one's descriptions be regularized? Consistency, a quality so closely resembling virtue that one should always practise it, has its place. It will be a modest one. Something can be achieved through elegance of grouping – Yorkists, conspirators, Ardenites and visitors. But the challenge is atomistic. Here is an individual human being, who rises above the faceless ranks of soldiers, courtiers, and so on. That individual has a name and some sort of social coding. What is there that can usefully be said, within short compass?

The virtues of a dramatis personae I take to be accuracy, coupled with caution, and conciseness, coupled with fulness. I think the conciseness-fulness spectrum is the best place to start, since a willingness to accept expansion pre-empts some difficulties.

1. Consider H. J. Oliver's single-text Oxford edition of *The Taming of the Shrew* (1984), which offers 'LUCENTIO, from Pisa, a younger suitor, eventually Bianca's husband; for much of the time disguised as CAMBIO, a teacher of languages.' This is growing into a passable c.v. With an entry for 'club' and 'recreations,' it might serve for *Who's Who*. Even so, the description says nothing about Lucentio's own identity (a gentleman?) nor does it mention his father, Vincentio. The entry is at once bloated and emaciated. The Complete Oxford has a condensed version, 'LUCENTIO, from Pisa, who disguises himself as Cambio, a teacher.' Evidently, the later principle is that disguise identity is proper to a dramatis personae, but not a marital transformation. Today's tendency, I suspect, is towards ever fuller description. A clear proof is David Bevington's 1986 edition of *Henry IV, Part One* in the Oxford series, which

invites comparison with the treatment of the same play in his 1980 text. The later dramatis personae is altogether fuller. The Earl of Westmoreland, for example, listed without comment in 1980, is in 1986 'loyal to the king' (a suggestion of soap opera updatings, one feels). 'HENRY, PRINCE OF WALES, *son of the King*' (1980) becomes 'PRINCE HENRY, Prince of Wales, also called Hal and Harry, King Henry's eldest son and heir.' (1986) This is no doubt helpful, if redundant, since the Prince of Wales is necessarily the eldest son and heir. I presume that the unacknowledged principle here is to give college students as much information as possible, even at the cost of prolixity.

The borderline between fulness and prolixity will call for delicate judgment. It is, I think, a useful innovation for the Oxford to list Bertram's mother as 'The Dowager COUNTESS OF ROUSSILLION,' the extra word clearing up her status *vis-a-vis* her daughter-in-law. On the other hand, this form of listing might seem to invite the treatment of Helena as 'COUNTESS OF ROUSSILLION.' After all, Helena's marriage to Bertram is not an Act 5 terminus to the comedy, but an Act 2 climax that generates most of the play's action. In fact, the Oxford gives 'HELEN, an orphan, attending on the Countess,' which makes no reference to her marriage to Bertram. Should it? There is a natural tendency for the plot to encroach upon the dramatis personae, which probably needs to be resisted. Even so, it is not clear why disguise identities should be admitted to the dramatis personae (Rosalind/Ganymede, Celia/Aliena), while a marital transformation is excluded. As for Helena's standing at the beginning of the play, the Oxford rather dodges the issue. Most people become orphans at some time or other; it is not the most helpful of categories. Russell Fraser in the New Cambridge *All's Well That Ends Well* (1985), Bevington, and the Riverside all offer 'HELENA, a gentlewoman, protected by the Countess,' which says what needs to be said about Helena's Act 1 status without launching into the plot.

2. The main requirement must always be accuracy. On occasion, this entails a conservative description; the editor says less than he might. T. W. Craik, in his New Arden edition of *Twelfth Night* (1975), registers Sir Toby Belch as *Olivia's kinsman*. He offers an extensive note, based on Dover Wilson's argument: 'The word "uncle" does not appear in the play, and though Olivia is often called his "niece" this is a vaguer term in Shakespeare's day than ours and she herself addresses him as "cousin", a vaguer term still . . .'[5] I think myself that the number of times 'niece' is spoken, by various people, takes the term out of the realm of social ambiguity; and Olivia may well be disinclined to address Sir Toby as 'uncle,' which creates a heightened and perhaps false sense of the relationship between them. Still, this is clearly legitimate caution, which Bevington and the Riverside override with *uncle to Olivia*. The Oxford is perhaps over-confident in identifying Valeria (in *Coriolanus*) as 'a chaste lady of Rome.' Is the moral testimony of one's friends a sufficient guarantor for dramatis personae? The Riverside and Bevington are on safer grounds with *friend to Virgilia*. Then there is the standing of Montano in *Othello*. Almost all editors, including the Oxford, Bevington, and New Cambridge (1984) list him as *Governor of Cyprus*. But M. R. Ridley in his New Arden edition (1958) preferred the more circumspect *Othello's predecessor in the government of Cyprus*, a description that goes back to the 1681 quarto. I think Ridley is right: everything about Montano suggests that he is an acting appointment, 'Your trusty and most valiant servitor' as the Messenger calls him (1.3.41). He is neither recalled upon the arrival of Othello nor reinstated following Othello's disgrace and death. In a diplomatic context, Montano would be understood as a chargé d'affaires; as his standing is military, he is simply the senior officer in the Cyprus garrison, pending the arrival of the General (or Governor-General) and his staff.[6]

3. We come to more substantive matters of rank, which

bear upon that most vexed of Elizabethan social issues, those above and below the line. Vincentio in *The Taming of the Shrew* is a convenient starting-point. Editors are unaccountably loath to identify his social standing. The Oxford lists him as 'Lucentio's father,' as does H. J. Oliver in the Oxford single-text edition. Brian Morris, in his New Arden edition (1981), gives *rich citizen of Pisa, father to Lucentio.* (In the same list, Lucentio is *a gentleman of Pisa*: why does not Lucentio take on the same rank as his father?) Ann Thompson's New Cambridge edition (1984) makes Vincentio *a rich old citizen of Pisa – father to Lucentio.* Dover Wilson and Bevington avert their eyes from the fact of Vincentio's wealth, as does the Riverside. None makes the basic attribution. Vincentio is a *merchant*, as Lucentio tells us:

> Pisa, renownèd for grave citizens
> Gave me my being, and my father first –
> A merchant of great traffic through the world,
> Vincentio, come of the Bentivolii.

(1.1.10–13)

I do not see why editors should be more discreet than the sons of dramatis personae.

Why does *merchant* matter? Obviously, because it is the basic category of occupation/rank; less obviously, because it affects the question of social standing in relation to *gentleman*. The one does not guarantee the other. John Russell Brown, in his New Arden edition of *The Merchant of Venice* (1955) quotes Coryat: 'The Rialto . . . is a most stately building, being the Exchange of Venice, where the Venetian Gentlemen and the Merchants doe meete twice a day.' (p. 22) Gentlemen and merchants: that will do nicely as an anticipation of a later English coding, Gentlemen and Players. In *The Taming of the Shew*, though, the distinction is not far from the surface. The New Arden edition, when it first appeared in 1981, wrongly listed Baptista Minola as *a rich merchant*. This was later changed to *a rich citizen of Padua*. Baptista thinks of himself as a gentleman ('Was ever gentleman thus grieved as I?' 2.1.37), and is so regarded by others: he is 'an affable and courteous gentleman' (Hortensio, 1.2.97), and 'a noble gentleman' (Tranio, 2.1.240). Baptista's sole reference to the merchant class indicates that he is not of it:

> Faith, gentlemen, now I play a merchant's part,
> And venture madly on a desperate mart.

> (2.1.322–23)

A merchant, in this value-system, is one who takes risks: a gentleman, as is Baptista (and Petruchio) does not need to. He thrives through the objective certainties of inheritance, marriage, and dowry. It has been well said that in England – which is, it goes without saying, the locale of *The Taming of the Shrew* – the genteel is risk-averse.

There is a certain roughness to the social styles of 'Padua,' but the term 'gentleman' is freely used in the dialogue and it covers all the leading male personages. However, the Oxford, while according the title to Petruchio and Baptista, withholds it from the others. Lucentio is merely 'from Pisa, who disguises himself as Cambio, a teacher,' while Vincentio, from whom we might expect more social guidance, is limply registered as 'Lucentio's father.' The buck passes to and fro. After this bureaucratic shuffling of identities, the reader is left to make up his own mind. This reader considers that Lucentio's standing is that of *Vincentio's son*, and that Vincentio is *a rich merchant of Pisa*.

I have skirted around the distinction between *gentleman* and *citizen*, not with the aim of avoiding this sensitive area, but so that it can be treated in its proper English context: *The Merry Wives of Windsor*. Here, the Oxford faces up to its responsibilities and groups the Pages and Fords under 'Citizens of Windsor.' In this it follows Dover Wilson and H. J. Oliver's New Arden edition of 1971. The description reflects the *OED* sense of *citizen*, 'esp. one possessing civic rights and privileges, a burgess or freeman of a city.' Bevington decides on a crucial social promotion, listing Page and Ford as *two gentlemen dwelling at Windsor*, an attribution for which he may plead the dubious authority of Rowe. The Riverside also sees Page and Ford as *gentlemen of Windsor*. The difficulty is the juxtaposition of the Pages with Fenton, who is unquestionably a *gentleman* ('young,' too, as the Oxford allows). Page 'doth object I am too great a birth' complains Fenton, without however disputing the social coding. (3.4.4) The Bystander in *Pygmalion* resolved these matters tersely: 'he's a gentleman: look at his boots.' The student of Elizabethan drama will pay more attention to blank verse, generally a sign that the speaker is at least capable of assimilation into the social ranks above the line. In a predominantly prose play, Fenton speaks verse nearly all the time (save with Mistress Quickly in a scene of low political bargaining, 1.4); the Pages speak verse occasionally. Page and Ford are well-heeled burghers, and the mating of Fenton and Anne Page follows a pattern on view elsewhere in Shakespeare, most notably in *Romeo and Juliet*. It is an alliance between the only daughter of the moneyed bourgeoisie, and the scion of a gentle, perhaps aristocratic house. Hence it is misleading to close the social gap between the Pages and Fenton by listing both as *gentlemen*. Neither Ford nor Page would object to the term, but the most accurate choice for an editor is *citizen*. The *Merry Wives of Windsor* is a play about people besotted with upward mobility, but an editor is not obliged to acquiesce in their aspirations.

The failure to discriminate between social ranks is marked in *Much Ado About Nothing*, where the Oxford repeats a venerable error. Benedick and Claudio are listed as 'lords, companions of Don Pedro.' Claudio is certainly a lord. The Messenger refers to him as 'the right noble Claudio' (1.1.79–80), and he later emerges as 'Count Claudio.' Benedick is not. He is always referred to as 'Signor Benedick,' never with a title of nobility. When Don Pedro addresses Claudio and Benedick as 'Signor Claudio and Signor Benedick' (1.1.140–41), this is no more than a tactful evening of modes. (It is in the same breath that Don Pedro refers to 'my dear friend Leonato.' Translation: 'among friends we can drop strict protocol.') Benedick, then, should be designated *a gentleman*, against Claudio *a young lord*. The social formation anticipates Parolles and Bertram. During the crisis of Act 4, the alliance between nobles holds firm, while Beatrice detaches Benedick from them; and she does so with an outburst of social hostility that would be strange indeed if Benedick were included among the enemy. 'Princess and counties! Surely a princely testimony, a goodly count, Count Comfit, a sweet gallant, surely.' (4.1.316–18) Beatrice's basic question is: whose side are you on? At the core of *Much Ado About Nothing* is a certain class tension, as well as the much-rehearsed emotional plight of Beatrice. The overwhelming impression that playgoers and readers receive is that Beatrice and Benedick are of essential parity, in social class as in other matters. It is the business of an accurate dramatis personae to register this parity.

Social rank is the standard to which a dramatis personae must address itself, however much the issues may be finessed through such expedients as 'son of,' 'wife to,' 'friend of.' It is easy to prolong a series of neutral descriptions: in the Oxford, Antonio is 'a merchant of Venice,' Bassanio is 'his friend and Portia's suitor,' and Gratiano is listed among 'friends of Antonio and Bassanio.' Perfectly true, all of it. And nothing tells us about Gratiano as hanger-on to Lord

Bassanio, and Bassanio as the aristocratic recipient of favours from his merchant friend in the City. Between the garrulousness of editors who want to tell us about the plot, and the impenetrable discretion of editors who want to say as little as possible about the social standing of the characters, the current dramatis personae listings oscillate.

And yet the task of social identification remains. Normally, not invariably, a Shakespeare character will have a core of social coding which is capable of discovery and identification – and, if necessary, of translation. Even so, a degree of social ambiguity may be present. *A Midsummer Night's Dream* is instructive. In Act 5, lines which in the Quarto are spoken by Philostrate are in the Folio reassigned to Egeus. One would not say that Egeus is very like Philostrate; and the actor who is assigned 'Philostrate' will characteristically play him on a different note from 'Egeus.' He can drop the suppressed irascibility, for one thing. But this instance is presumably a matter of theatrical exigence. There is another dimension, for social ambiguity is normal in life and must be admitted to the stage. Malvolio's standing as 'gentleman' is not confirmed until the final stages of *Twelfth Night*, and yet it must inform the actor (and the attitudes of other members of Olivia's household). As it happens, this is not a problem for the dramatis personae, since editors always list Malvolio as *steward*. But the instance is a warning that one may be well advised to leave a space around a character when it comes to dramatis personae listing.

The dramatis personae must list the actors in ways that are faithful to the text and to history, yet are open to a modern reader. Of necessity, there will have to be some editorial juggling with categories, and some licence. It is tempting to see the modern editor as a director manqué, casting his actors in eclectic garb. The editor is bound to feel some intellectual discomfort at this jostling of headboroughs and gentlemen, stewards and whores. Is *lady* an

anachronism? Are *citizens, gentlemen*? Salvation cannot lie
in a return to Old Spelling historicism; editors began to
evacuate that redoubt a decade ago and more. Nowadays
only a handful of Landwehr defend it. Modernization, then?
But modernization is what we are supposed to have, and
the present simply lacks, or prefers not to employ, some
categories of the past. The steady neutralization of the present
by the past does not admit of energetic policies. Editors
might as well admit, as stage directors do, that 'Theatrically,
[consistent] period costume is an outmoded convention,'[7]
and resign themselves to dramatis personae as costume
drama, the social register of a fancy dress ball. Motley's the
only wear.

10

Measure for Measure: Casting the Star

What is the star part for a male actor? Extraordinary in this as in other issues, *Measure for Measure* gives a shifting answer to the simplest of questions. It is hard to be equivocal over the standing of the major Shakespearean parts; the ratings are confirmed on an exchange over four centuries. One might shade one or two ratings, certainly. Julius Caesar is probably considered a rather better part than in the past – a miniaturized major role, rather than a decent middle-order role. An actor might fairly hesitate between Laertes and Horatio,[1] or choose Caliban over Prospero. But these are marginalia. One knows where one stands. All the more astonishing, then, is the shift in *Measure for Measure*. The thesis is that the star part used to be Angelo, and now, from the early 1970s, is the Duke. This thesis is stated with exemplary clarity by Adrian Noble of the RSC, in interview. 'When I first saw *Measure for Measure*, here in Stratford in 1970 – John Barton's production – the leading character was Angelo, without doubt. Nowadays the leading character is either Isabella or the Duke – probably the Duke.'[2]

Isabella does not, I think, give us a problem here. The role is vibrant with feminine issues, but then it always has been; and there is no female competition. Mrs Siddons used to play the part until, grown bulky with age, she had to be assisted to her feet by her co-kneelers. It is the male parts which have carried the energies of the times, and where the leading conductor has switched from Angelo to Vincentio. The matter can conveniently be assessed from 1950 to the present day, and the primary need is to clarify the standing of the actors playing Angelo and the Duke.

This is neither difficult nor invidious. In 1950, Peter Brook's production at Stratford-upon-Avon assigned Angelo to John Gielgud. A great actor in his prime, Gielgud was the star of Stratford in the 1950 season: his other roles were Cassius, Benedick, King Lear. He unquestionably chose in Angelo the role he wanted, a study in sexual repression. The reviews reflected the priority of the casting. *The Times* gave the Duke a single line, 'Mr Harry Andrews is a decorative Duke.'[3] And the *Birmingham Mail* allowed him half a sentence: 'Harry Andrews gave an impression of pleasant probity and . . .'[4] Even this was ampler than the parenthesis which the *Evening Standard* accorded to the Duke, '(excellently played by Harry Andrews)'.[5] Radical as Brook's production was, it never questioned the priority of casting.

Nor did the next *Measure for Measure* at Stratford, Anthony Quayle's production in 1956. This time Angelo was played by Emlyn Williams, the 'allowed star' of the season whose other parts were Shylock and Iago. Again, the reviews reflected this sense of hierarchy. *The Times* all but ignored Anthony Nicholls' 'manly' Duke,[6] and 'a resonant and effective Duke' was all the *Financial Times* could say.[7] The play was easily viewed as 'a poetic thesis in sexual ethics,' as Kenneth Young put it.[8] But here there are signs of the play's intractable nature troubling the reviewers. 'Anthony Nicholls only momentarily becomes the symbol of the loving God *which Shakespeare surely intended.*'[9] [My italics.] The *Oxford Mail*, however, referred to the Duke as 'that unholy confidence trickster.'[10] Here is the schism whose history is so well traced by Jane Williamson, between the view of Vincentio as God's Vice-Regent and as venal fraud.[11]

The doctrine of 'unripe time' must have prevailed, though,

and no full-scale assault on the Duke was mounted in the 1960s. The only Stratford production of *Measure for Measure* was John Blatchley's, in 1962. Marius Goring, who played Angelo – his only Stratford engagement that season – was the leading actor, and got most of the reviewing space. His 'sincere puritan'[12] focused a traditional view of the play. Tom Fleming was not greatly admired as Vincentio, and *The Times* found him 'an adventurous opportunist.'[13] But J. C. Trewin's sense of the options is notable. 'Whether we consider him to be "power divine," or as a ruler thinking up specious excuses for what seems to have been fairly casual misgovernment . . .'[14] Still, Fleming's Duke had not crumbled under the questioning of the times, and Philip Hope-Wallace saw him as 'proving his point with the vigour of a great moralist.'[15]

All this changed in the pivotal year, 1970. John Barton's RSC *Measure for Measure* did indeed continue the tradition of making Angelo the star. Ian Richardson, whose parts that year included Buckingham, Prospero, Proteus, and Ford, was then close to the peak of his distinguished association with the RSC, and his Angelo was a sharply-etched authoritarian. Sebastian Shaw made Vincentio into a well-meaning but slightly gauche figure. 'In appearance, with his Holbein cap and spectacles, he suggests a university vice-chancellor: a paternal administrator whose encouraging smiles are always contracting into icy severity.'[16] But the dénouement changed all previous values. Estelle Kohler's Isabella failed to accept the Duke's hand in marriage: she was left alone on stage, obviously bewildered and disturbed. I can find no record of such a reaction in any previous production. The stroke was original, though in accord with the logic of the times. Isabella's resistance to the Duke has overshadowed (though not governed) all subsequent productions; but it did not in 1970 disturb the tradition of casting priorities. That step, logical and inevitable, came in 1974 with the next RSC *Measure for Measure*. Barrie Ingham as Vincentio ranked senior to Michael Pennington as Angelo, and this signalled the full-frontal new *Measure for Measure*. Keith Hack's production was much reviled: he projected the Duke as 'a narcissistic voluptuary'[17] and 'a morally discredited fraud wearing the mask of justice.'[18] The same reviewer found Vienna to be Brecht's Mahagonny, and saw Angelo as 'virile and supercilious.' The end found Francesca Annis's Isabella tense, angry, and trapped as her fate closed in on her, and one reviewer at least was sympathetic: 'a single night of shame with Angelo would have been a kinder fate than marriage to this satanic rapist.'[19] All this was hard for many in the audience to take. But the concept is entirely defensible, and Richard David defended it. 'Hack had seized upon the fact that a modern audience is liable to find the Duke incredible and Isabella odious.'[20] What Hack's extremist production did was to abandon the assumption that Angelo is the leading part, chosen by or assigned to the leading available actor. If the Duke is potentially among the villains, he becomes more interesting, playable, desirable. His motives are buried in a shallow grave: why not disinter them? Does *any* actor not wish to play the villain?

This does not, of course, mean that Angelo has been permanently demoted to Part No. 2. Rather, the casting of the two leads seems now an open question, to be settled without preconception on the basis of available company strength. Jonathan Miller's 1975 production at Greenwich balanced the interest between Julian Curry's Angelo – bureaucratic, legalistic, fastidious – and Joseph O'Conor's Duke:

> Mr O'Conor cuts an entirely convincing figure as elder statesman and father confessor; so convincing indeed, whether acting benevolently or with inexplicable cruelty, that realization dawns that he is the biggest seemer of the lot. At which point the moral centre drops out of the drama.[21]

Penelope Wilton's Isabella explicitly refused this Duke: 'At the Duke's proposal, she backs away from him in nerveless horror, plainly heading for the convent never to re-emerge.'[22] In the same vein, Robin Phillips's production at Stratford, Ontario in the same year balanced the interest between William Hutt (Canada's leading classical actor) as Duke, and Brian Bedford, one of North America's outstanding actors, as Angelo. Here again Isabella (Martha Henry), torn with doubts, was unable to accept the Duke's proposal. The mid-seventies concept was of a Duke whose motives were scrutinized with growing scepticism; Angelo, being a Scarpia-type scoundrel to start with, could offer no comparable basis for re-examination. Hence one could make something striking and new of the Duke, and this offered obvious attractions to the actor best positioned to seize the part.

Subsequent productions have backed off the claim that Vincentio is a moral leper, or at least a fraud. Instead they are prepared to find him benevolent but confused. In 1978, Michael Pennington – who had moved up in the RSC ranks – played Vincentio in Barry Kyle's production, to Jonathan Pryce's Angelo. Pennington struck the authentic contemporary note, as J. C. Trewin detected: 'He acts a man long debated and troubled by the problems of authority.'[23] *Authority*: that is the pole towards which the needle swings. The 1978 production was perfectly prepared to endorse this puzzled liberal humanist, and Paola Dionisotti's Isabella accepted him at once, at the first proposal. With some reservations, a similar endorsement emerged from the next RSC *Measure for Measure*, Adrian Noble's 1983 production. Here the Duke was played by Daniel Massey, who had recently starred at the National Theatre and was evidently the leading actor. His motives were enigmatic but benign, and Irving Wardle found that 'Mr Massey dwindles into a wry humanist.'[24] Juliet Stevenson's Isabella felt able to accept him at the end. (Nowadays, no Duke can hope to escape a considered appraisal.) The Vincentio-Isabella equation was not disturbed by David Schofield's study of Angelo as 'a jumped-up place seeker and mercenary exploiter of women.'[25] Clearly, the Duke was the major casting, and the *New Statesman* notes that Daniel Massey took a solo bow at the end.[26] That would have seemed strange to an earlier generation of playgoers.

We are left with the most recent RSC exposition of the play, Nicholas Hytner's production in 1987.[27] Here again Vincentio went with Company seniority, to Roger Allam. The Duke was discovered in a state bordering on the catatonic. He had lost the capacity even to sign official documents, and his loss of confidence and self-belief was the production's keynote. Eric Shorter quite reasonably found that the Duke 'seems to be mentally ill at the start of the play.'[28] Hence the production's 'super-objective' was to show the 'demi-god, authority' racked with doubt concerning its own legitimacy. Sean Baker's Angelo could not influence this sense of the play. At the end, Josette Simon's Isabella failed to endorse the Duke; she neither refused nor accepted him, but exited with a wary and considering look. Authority was still on probation.

It is evident that authority has now replaced sex as the central issue of *Measure for Measure*, and that the casting priority follows this sense of the play's values. Naturally one does not erect this observation into a prediction. Sex can scarcely wither away like the Marxist state. It may be, as Adrian Noble thought, that repressed sexuality is less interesting to audiences today, presumably because there is less of it around; but the sexual nitroglycerine in the Isabella–Angelo encounters can never be other than high-tension theatre, enormously thrilling to actors and audiences. Conversely, one cannot count on authority's future as the butt of RSC productions. The RSC – which, as Kenneth Tynan used to observe, is composed of Roundheads against the National Theatre's Cavaliers – has its own reasons for giving authority a hard time, at least during the 1980s. One can conceive easily of a time when the image of a benign liberal humanist, bending his efforts towards social harmony and open to the need for greater arts funding, might be more appealing to the RSC's directorate. At present, though, the play's essence remains contentious and debatable, but viewed often as subversive to authority. The gainer is clearly the actor playing the Duke, whose range of possibilities has widened strikingly. It is less clear that the loser is Angelo: or for long.

11

Within the Bermuda Triangle: Reflections on Recent *Tempests*

In the late summer/fall of 1988, four productions of *The Tempest* were on view virtually at the same time in England: Sir Peter Hall's at the National Theatre, with Michael Bryant as Prospero; Jonathan Miller's at the Old Vic, with Max von Sydow; Declan Donnellan's Cheek by Jowl company, with Timothy Walker; and Nicholas Hytner's for the RSC, with John Wood. These productions, all of a high order, show *The Tempest* as remaining in the inner repertory of Shakespeare, that part of the canon most charged with meaning today. But there is no single aspect of these productions that calls attention to itself as new, as radically changed from the recent past. Stage history can evolve through a striking new production that changes our perception of the play – Peter Brook's *King Lear* (RSC, 1962), say, or Peter Hall's *Henry V* (RSC, 1964). More often though meanings will change gradually over the years, with no outstanding production to which one can point as a milestone. This is so with *The Tempest*. There is not, I believe, a single production in the past generation that could be described as 'revolutionary'; and yet our sense of the play in performance has changed greatly. Hence I want to offer not a collective review of the major productions of 1988, but some reflections on the play's essences as they now appear on stage. They appear above all in the casting and playing of the three main parts, and the relationships within this triangle.

I. CALIBAN

The twentieth-century history of Caliban is a sustained movement to bring him within the ambit of civilized society. To the Victorians, he was a figure of loathing and repulsion, a monster against whom society's resource was exclusion. Benson used regularly to play Caliban hanging upside-down from the branches of a tree, gibbering.[1] That would not be possible today; and the modern view begins to edge into view with Beerbohm Tree's highly sympathetic portrayal (1904), ending with the famous tableau of Caliban alone on his island peering after the departing Milanese and Neapolitans. More recent Calibans have been grotesque, unlikeable, repellent. But all start from the premise that Caliban has a case, which must be given a hearing, and that some prospect of his readmission into society must be entertained. For actors and the general audience, extreme penalties for attempted rape and attempted murder are not to be imposed.

A strategic technicality is the assignment of the speech

> Abhorred slave,
> Which any print of goodness wilt not take

> (1.2.353–54)

to Prospero or Miranda. Editors used until modern times to assign the speech to Prospero, overriding the Folio. They did this on the grounds that the speech was out of character for the passive, feminine Miranda, and much more in keeping with Prospero. The reasoned conservatism of today's editors does not incline them to amend the Folio without good cause; and they are much more ready to see in this energetic speech another side to Miranda, rather than a fault of transmission. She is her father's daughter, after all. On stage, my impression is that directors also prefer to assign the speech to Miranda. This decision sketches in the beginnings of a relationship between Miranda and Caliban, in which she has tried to teach him; it hints at a plea on behalf of Caliban's later behaviour, presenting the core of the attempted rape as amorous rather than a revenge upon Prospero. Thus the contingent nature of evil is suggested, and the worst aspect of Caliban is softened if not condoned.

The identity of the contemporary Caliban is what now concerns us. I can see two categories. The first is colonial, or historical: on this reading, Caliban must fit in to the history of the white man and the ethnic groups who have contested his imperial expansion. This is easily done on stage, and a few instances will suffice. Peter Hall (National Theatre, 1974) gave his Caliban, Denis Quilley, a Mohican look. Ron Daniels' RSC revival (1983) gave Bob Peck the suggestion of a Rastafarian haircut.[2] Jonathan Miller's notable Mermaid production of 1970 presented both Caliban and Ariel as blacks in a colonial island shortly before Independence: Caliban was the detribalized, dispossessed field hand, Ariel the clever house boy sure to do well in the administration after independence.[3] These castings illustrate an assumption of the 1960s and 1970s, that one could easily read *The Tempest* in terms of colonialism, as a parable for the times. But this reading is less popular today. I suspect that directors have become bored with Caliban as a victim of colonial oppression. Nothing frightens a director so much as the imputation of cliché or stereotype. It is true that Jonathan Miller retained the dual black casting for his Old Vic revival of 1988. Even so, the colonial framework is a constriction of the play, which may have outlived its usefulness.

The alternative category is anthropoid. In this, Caliban escapes from the allusion to history. Indeed, a director such as Peter Brook, who formally repudiates history as a context for his productions and has never directed a Shakespeare history play, can scarcely do other than turn away from direct reference. It is easy, vulgar, and therefore disgusting.

Caliban as some kind of outcast from the human race, who is nonetheless not without an appealing aspect, is a more inviting prospect.

A telling survey of the options involved can be found in David Suchet's experience with the role. After being cast as Caliban for Clifford Williams's production (RSC, 1978). Suchet describes how he came to terms with the part.[4] He spent much time on the monster/man fissure, before opting for the man. The key line became '*This is no fish, but an islander*' (2.2.35–36). Williams's first thought was that Caliban might be 'half-fish, half-man (presumably I would wear fins) or possibly something deformed . . .'[5] Eventually 'I wanted to look like "basic man" and I wanted to be of a blackish hue. But I didn't want to be instantly recognizable as being obviously an African native or an Indian or an Eskimo or an Aborigine.'[6] Suchet's instincts took him away from a clear frame of allusion, with a direct reference to a specific people or episode. Instead, he went for eclecticism. Eclecticism is a ruling principle of today's stage, and its ramifications are endless. What it means here is that Calibans do not need to approach the part with a logical finality, nor need we.

The 'anthropoid' category – which is large, loose, and convenient – has easy relations with pop culture. There are numerous generic models to which Caliban can be linked, openly or subliminally. The films of Spielberg and Lucas specialize in creatures that are non-human, but have an easily-grasped human identity. Again, gorillas have recently re-asserted their hold over the human imagination. (*Gorillas in the Mist.*) This is an enduring theme, as Alec Clunes' ape-man Caliban in Peter Brook's production (Stratford-upon-Avon, 1957) shows.[7] In this pop-cultural hinterland is Tarzan, and the circle of Kipling's Mowgli. Common to all these models is the sympathetic partisanship of the animal or non-human world. Directors, who are also politicians, want to maximize support from the Animal Liberation Front and kindred movements. On the ultra-grotesque side, *The Elephant Man* has lodged its message: 'I am a human being.' This message structures the deformities and alien qualities of Caliban. Generally, the anthropoid Caliban will put forth an appeal that may border upon charm. And this quality is retained with those Calibans who are not anthropoid but fully human. Declan Donnellan, whose Cheek by Jowl Caliban was entirely human, insisted that Caliban 'is very attractive and consequently very dangerous.'[8]

Caliban, in brief, is the outsider who can generate some sympathy and regard in the audience. The apotheosis of the contemporary Caliban may well have been reached in an agency photograph that went around the world in October 1988. Her Majesty Queen Elizabeth II visited the National Theatre, to see Sir Peter Hall's production of *The Tempest*, and there met the actors. In the photograph, Caliban (Tony Haygarth) is being introduced to the Queen. He is naked save for a sumo wrestler's loincloth combined with a most noble codpiece of arresting dimensions; and he is dark stained. There are no grotesque distortions to his face. He has clearly retained for the occasion the rough and manly charm that distinguished his performance. (The same actor had a comparable success as Cloten in the same company's *Cymbeline*: there is a cross-fertilizing humour in the castings.) Caliban, one might say, has been received into society at the highest level. His sins are symbolically forgiven.

I have been describing a stage phenomenon, as it is linked to the outside world of ideas and values. There is some lexical evidence that catches the same drift. 'Caliban' is a name that is recognized in the dictionaries; and the *OED* contains the unmistakable flavor of the nineteenth-century Caliban, with (after the derivation) 'thence applied to a man of degraded bestial nature.' The citations include George Eliot: 'Grandcourt held that the Jamaica negro was a beastly sort of baptist Caliban.' (*Daniel Deronda* [1876] iv.xxix) *Webster's Third New International Dictionary* (1961) offers 'a person or thing that is or is felt to be [note the qualification] slavish, brutal, monstrous, or deformed.' But the *Random House* (2nd edition, 1987) offers only 'the ugly, beastlike slave of Prospero in Shakespeare's *The Tempest*', which is distinctly milder. In the same vein is *Chambers 20th Century Dictionary* (1983), which has only 'a man of beastly nature, from the monster of that name in Shakespeare's *Tempest*.' The current meaning is beginning to cast off its origin-moorings. The concentrated essence of loathing, so plain in the Eliot citation, is diluted over the years.

Caliban is the beneficiary of a tidal movement of twentieth century thought. He is now perceived as the underdog, as the underprivileged, as the exploited.[9] In his contention with his master (of which more later) Caliban is seen as the victim of authoritarian and repressive tendencies. The play will not, for a modern audience, be premised on Prospero being right and Caliban being wrong. I do not myself justify this position, or its opposite: I am describing what is happening. Caliban's final position sounds a note that will be familiar to the audience. He receives a suspended sentence for conspiracy to murder, coupled with some token community service.

II.   ARIEL

The main point to grasp is Ariel's sex-change. Ariel, of course, started out as a male role, of necessity. 'By the early eighteenth century,' Stephen Orgel tells us, 'Ariel . . . had become exclusively a woman's role, usually taken by a singer who was also a dancer, and so it remained until the 1930s.'[10] Throughout the Victorian era and well into the twentieth century Ariel was normally – I believe, invariably – played by an actress. Leslie French, in the Old Vic production of 1930, was the first male Ariel of modern times; and for some years afterwards the casting was an open directorial choice.

This intermediary period lasted at least until 1952, when Margaret Leighton was the last actress to play Ariel at Stratford-upon-Avon. (Even so, Elvi Hale played Ariel in 1983 at St George's, admittedly a theatre with a conservative tradition.) We can get an idea of the female, mid-century Ariel from the photograph of Rachel Kempson in the part at Stratford-upon-Avon, 1934.[11] Ariel is simply a very pretty girl in tights, with a strong generic hint of pantomime. The underground identity of the female mid-century Ariel seems obvious: she is the Principal Boy.

Of recent years, actresses have pulled out of this kind of engagement. We expect to see Ariel – and Puck, and Chorus in *Henry V* – played by a male actor, and almost invariably do. Whatever degree of sexual titillation is implied in the casting of Ariel is now switched to a different track. The development of Ariel in the last generation as an exclusively male preserve has contained two aspects, perhaps two phases. In the first, Ariel is an androgyne. This fey, pallid creature exists outside any recognizable sexual identity, save that of the coquette. ('Do you love me, master? No?') In the second, Ariel is decidedly male, sometimes aggressively so. Of this type, Ian Charleson's Ariel (RSC, 1978) remains outstanding, a shop steward intensely concerned with overtime benefits, anti-social hours, and accelerated retirement clauses. On this view Ariel is above all a *worker*, a servant to Prospero who is well aware that the plant needs to be unionized (and in 1978, can be). On the sexual view,[12] Ariel remains in an ambiguous but charged relationship with his master. The male casting of Ariel has allowed a certain homoerotic tinge to the relationship, something no doubt present in the earliest performances of *The Tempest*. The underground story of the Prospero-Ariel relationship is often apparent in the playhouse, but is commonly not remarked on in the reviews.

The climax of the relationship is therefore reached at the point when Ariel inquires 'Do you love me, master? No?'

and Prospero admits 'Dearly, my delicate Ariel.' (4.1.48–49)
There is always one who loves and one who is loved. Ariel,
'were I human,' is secure in his detachment from the turbulence of human emotions. It is a quality often perceived as
coldness. The outcome is Ariel's realization that the master-
servant relationship is reversed, as in the film *The Servant*.
The Tempest is after all a revenge play, like all of Shakespeare's plays.

It remains to be added that there is virtually no relationship between Ariel and Caliban. Mutually hostile, they move
on separate tracks. Caliban wants the island, while Ariel
wants freedom. Ariel has read the works of Régis Debray;
Caliban just knows that you do it with a machete. Their
roles can be read easily enough in the later stages of the Raj
in India. Caliban is the mutineer, Ariel the temporary loyal-
ist who bids up an ever-increasing price for his services.
Prospero has to pay the price anyway. The accelerating pace
of independence takes on its own momentum, and he has
no choice.

III.   PROSPERO

To get at Prospero we shall have to set aside, courteously
but firmly, the rhetoric surrounding recent *Tempests*. If one
asks directors and actors what their intentions are, one is
likely to be entertained with a stereotype of incomprehension
against which truth-seekers are to contend. Prosperos, one
will be told, have habitually been played as serene old
men, tottering past golden ponds to their graves: in the new
Tempest will be seen a vital, younger Prospero, raging against
the world. Half of this is true. No doubt the ripest among us
can recall seeing a mellow Prospero. It has not fallen to my
lot since Alistair Sim tranquillized the part in 1962. (Since
Alistair Sim would have played Napoleon, Peer Gynt, and
Savonarola on the same note, there was nothing remark-

able in his usurpation of Prospero.) Prosperos today are, and have long been, unfailingly angry, disturbed, bitter. A couple of recent reviews catch the flavor. Michael Bryant's Prospero (National Theatre, 1988) is 'an impious magician devoured with hatred for the usurpers who have fallen into his power. Peremptory, urgent, and subject to fits of blind fury, Mr Bryant controls the events with matter-of-fact vigour, regularly exploding when anything dares to stand in his way.'[13] Jeremy Kingston writes of the 'seething rage' in John Wood's performance for the RSC.[14] Hatred and rage, clearly, are in. Why?

Actors approach the major parts nowadays at an earlier age than a generation and more ago. In this impatient era actors will commonly tackle the major parts as soon as they can, thus cutting out elders who have decorously but unwisely waited their turn in line. They have therefore much more energy and intensity to give to the part. Prospero will always be a role to attract an actor of mature years, like Max von Sydow in the Miller production, but I judge that recent par for the course is Derek Jacobi (RSC, 1982), and Len Cariou (Stratford, Ontario, 1982), who played the part at around forty. The text does not absolutely confirm Prospero to be an old man, and there is easy scope for muscular vigour.

But this is merely the physiology of casting. The main question remains on the table. I offer a short list of three answers, which could certainly be extended.

1. Anger is effective. The actor can always make a 'point' by relating a line to a sudden or prolonged gust of anger. It makes the audience sit up, it galvanizes the proceedings. Purely as a stage trick, there is much to recommend anger. Actors love it.

2. Anger is fashionable. It has long been banished from the Deadly Sins. The anger of Prospero hints at a moral under-pinning to his emotions. Who can admit to unrighteous anger? Since no one is angry without cause,

Prospero is making the case for himself in the most vehement way. He is tapping one of the mysterious themes of our time, the legitimization of anger.

3. Anger is ambivalent, not to be traced to a sure source. Prospero's feelings may be clarified by the director in interview or programme note, but on stage can be left unclear. Is he angry because deprived of his dukedom, or age, or thwarted designs upon Miranda? The text will not tell us. The director might. The actor won't, if he has any sense. The audience can be left to relate to this field of energy in terms of its own perceptions and preoccupations.

I should add that anger is not a guaranteed bonus to the actor. The cautionary tale of John Wood's Prospero has fabular resonance. During a preview at Stratford-upon-Avon (1988), he imprudently played in bare feet, the special footwear not having arrived from the makers. Stamping his foot with the peremptory vigour which we now associate with Prospero, he broke several bones in it and was out of the production for a couple of weeks. 'Prospero in plaster' was the company joke during that period. One sees that serenity has its privileges.

On the whole, though, serenity is a difficult property for Prospero to embrace. Few would care to admit possessing it. Wordsworth's view of old age, 'serene and lovely as a Lapland night,' does not get quoted as Dylan Thomas's is. Serenity might seem to claim a place in the moral spectrum running from hubris through smugness to stupidity. Besides, Prospero has problems which preclude serenity. Central to them is the loss of authority.

The text shows a man who has physical, but not moral power over the actions of the islanders. He controls their behavior, not their thoughts. But it is the minds, rather than the actions of his subjects that Prospero most wants to rule; he has therefore to admit a loss of authority in the area most ardently desired. The love of Ariel, the reform of Caliban, the repentance of Sebastian, even the decorous conduct of Miranda and Ferdinand – conduct which entails the moral responsibility of each, hence must be left outside Prospero's control – are not to be commanded. It can only be enjoined or invited. Hence there is an easy paradox in the text, that this all-powerful being is impotent in the issues that matter. This paradox has always to be inflected in performance, and it is clear that today's Prosperos are much more conscious of their loss of authority than ever before. But then, authority in general was socially sanctioned, a generation and more back, in ways that have now disappeared. Hence the current difficulty in portraying authority as authoritative. Nicholas Hytner's *Tempest* was preceded by the *Measure for Measure* (RSC, 1987) in which the Duke had lost all confidence in his role and values. I take Hytner's Duke to be a vector of a current stage problem, that one is going to look rather odd portraying authority in the mould of de Gaulle. Paradox moves towards contradiction, and then to anomaly. The outcome is a self-questioning of identity, a process most easily perceived as a crisis of patriarchy.

'Patriarchy' is a word in such ill odour that Prosperos have forgotten how to be patriarchs. John Wood often sat down on the stage boards, for all the world like an academic being determinedly unstuffy with his tutorial students and unwilling to admit that he does in fact hand out grades. To preserve authority and to preserve relationships, that is the problem for the liberal-academic Prospero. Simply, the role of patriarch is difficult, not only in itself but as a basis for communication with the audience. Actors, no less than Prospero, require to be loved; it is the moving principle of their profession. The intelligent exit from the problems is therefore to abdicate from the role; which is what, we can guess, would have been the solution of a great Prospero that never was, Olivier's. Peter Hall tells a revealing anecdote of his wooing of Olivier:

I rode home with Larry [Olivier] from a meeting at Max Rayne's and talked about *The Tempest* as the one play I wanted to do and the need for him to play Prospero. I pointed out that Prospero was acted traditionally by a remote old man – an aesthetic schoolmaster who was thinking of higher things, whereas Prospero should really be a man of power, of intelligence, as shrewd and cunning and egocentric as Churchill.

Larry listened. I think he was interested. He said he wanted to play the part for comedy, and that Prospero should lecture his daughter in the first scene while shaving. He said he couldn't wear all those whiskers and wigs Prosperos always wore.[15]

Which is to say, he declined the patriarch role. Olivier's instinct, working like a geiger-counter, had taken him directly to the problem area. It is a truth universally acknowledged, that a patriarch discovered shaving is in need of re-education.

The Tempest aspires always to the condition of allegory, and our experience of it will suggest fragments of a great allegory. These fragments cannot however be expected to cohere. Rather, there will be passages, foci, situations which are infused for a while with a personal and social energy; the energy then burns out, the passages become inert, and the energy is transferred elsewhere. The three leading personages and their relationships seem to pick up what is currently in the air, to attract the most gifted directors in their search for contemporary resonance. Caliban can be inflected towards the dispossessed, the alien, the criminal, the recalcitrant, the merely ugly – that is to say, those lacking the endowment of passable looks. Whatever his offences, the play acts for Caliban like a good lawyer and

gets a suspended sentence, together with an ambiguously-
phrased acknowledgment of responsibility from the ruling
spirit:

>   this thing of darkness I
> Acknowledge mine . . .
> He is as disproportion'd in his manners
> As in his shape. Go, sirrah, to my cell;
> Take with you your companions. As you look
> To have my pardon, trim it handsomely.

>   (5.1 278–79, 294–97)

Prospero, like the play, cannot condemn Caliban, and in the
end is reduced to shaking his head at Caliban's 'manners' as
though he were the Earl of Chesterfield lamenting his
blockish son. Ariel is a force operating along parallel lines,
the sexual and the subordinate. He wants not power, but
independence – or perhaps , power as a means of acquiring
independence. In production today, his final gesture is
often to disappear without indicating goodbye to Prospero.
That is his reward and his revenge. Prospero, desolated by
this desertion, is left commanding the (relatively unim-
portant) things that he can command, requiring his companions – it is the first time he says 'please' – 'please you
draw near,' and in the Epilogue beseeching the prayers of
the audience. The audience will have to determine what
relationship there is between the modern 'retirement' and
'retire me to my Milan.' Either meaning constitutes a re-
formation of 'authority.' Since Prospero has broken his
staff and forgiven his enemies, what more can he do? All
things considered, Prosperos might do worse than cultivate
a little serenity.

12

Falstaff's Space: The Tavern as Pastoral

When I first saw *Henry IV*, Part One, I found the Falstaff scenes entrancing and longed only for their renewal. The Court and political scenes I found rather tedious, and waited impatiently for Falstaff to come back. Thus my experience of the production was an alternation corresponding to the scenic pattern: the scenes in which Falstaff appeared, which were wholly delightful, and those in which the King and the rebels debated the future of the land, which I sat through with an indifference bordering on boredom. Later in my theatre-going experience I sought earnestly to modify this pattern of response, and looked for dramatic interest and political depth in the non-Falstaff scenes, qualities which the actors habitually failed to impart. Later still I came to the conclusion that my original responses were perfectly sound: the naive reaction is the correct one. As so often, of course.

If my sketch of the naive reaction is accepted, then I am not merely drawing attention to a banal feature of *Henry IV*, the fact that some scenes play better than others. I am describing the structure of the play as it affects the audience: it is a plan of organization, not a mere truism. It will be urged that this programming of performance does not govern all productions and all responses. That is true. All Shakespeare productions may yield unexpected areas outside the customary range. Conversely, certain scenes that are usually strong can be disappointing. Falstaffs can be undercast, like any other part. Similarly with the other major roles. Hotspur is usually considered a star part – but how many actors since Olivier and Redgrave have made a hit as Hotspur? I

141

doubt if there has been a really major Hal since Richard
Burton, and King Henry IV is not a part to tear a cat in. I
dare say that many of us have seen a Part One in which the
court-rebel scenes came flickeringly to life, and have lodged
in our memories. But the chances are that J. C. Trewin's
reflection will apply: 'Sometimes it can be a pity when he
[Falstaff] is so overwhelming that, in effect, the captains and
the kings depart.'[1] Falstaff is an outsize part, created as a
vehicle for a star actor. It will hardly be surprising that in
practice we respond more intensely to this star actor than to
any other element in the production. One arrives easily at a
subliminal judgment, that the political scenes are the price
we pay for the Falstaff scenes. That is it. There is a price, and
we pay it; perhaps a little reluctantly, but we have after all
no choice. It is the discipline, the inner necessity of the play.

But as soon as this thought breaks into consciousness, and is
formulated in words, we realize that *pay* (and its associated
terms *due, owe, reckoning*) is the manifest content of the play.
As a literal, *pay* is a staple of tavern talk. In the extended or
metaphoric sense it is the principle on which social action is
founded. *Pay*, a word unsurprisingly imported from France
and left to the English as a permanent legacy, is the nodal
term for *Henry IV*'s definition of morality. Hal does, Falstaff
doesn't. Their relations often fuse to a single question: who
pays?

This will be obvious enough, but the point is worth illus-
trating. Here are Falstaff and Hal in their first scene:

> *Prince* Why, what a pox have I to do with my hostess of
> the tavern?
> *Falstaff* Well, thou hast call'd her to a reckoning many a
> time and oft.
> *Prince* Did I ever call for thee to pay thy part?

Falstaff No; I'll give thee thy due, thou hast paid all
there.
Prince Yea, and elsewhere, so far as my coin would
stretch; and where it would not, I have us'd my
credit.

(1.2.46–54)

The Prince makes it delicately plain that his attachment to
Keynesian economics is not unlimited. Falstaff's enthusi-
asm for recycling debts – his own, above all – would never,
until fairly recent times, have made him a favorite of the
bankers. Again, take the tavern scene of 3.3, which contains
an unseemly brawl between the Hostess and Falstaff, with
the reiterated 'You owe me money, Sir John,' 'You owe
money here besides, Sir John, for your diet, and by-drinkings,
and money lent you, four and twenty pound.' (3.3.66–75)
This receives only the rigorous doctrine of 'He had his part
of it; let him pay.' Peace or war, the principle is the same;
and when the warlike Falstaff, like himself, orders his subordinate Bardolph to 'fill me a bottle of sack' at Coventry,
Bardolph's plaintive 'Will you give me money, captain?'
evokes only 'Lay out, lay out' (that is, pay out of your own
pocket). It is the same in Part Two, with another distressing
scene between Hostess and Falstaff (2.1), based on Falstaff's
'What is the gross sum that I owe thee?' (82) and the Hostess's claim that Sir John made various deep pledges to her.
Only in the final scene does Falstaff come out with the most
amazing line in the entire role: 'Master Shallow, I owe you
a thousand pound.' (5.5.73) But that is in shock. A moment
later, Shallow's suggestion of a 100 per cent repayment
programme is turned aside with 'That can hardly be, Master Shallow.' (77) Falstaff's principle of life is most accu-
rately caught by Pistol, who has clearly been listening to his
leader's table-talk: 'Base is the slave that pays.' (*Henry V*,
2.1.96)

So far I have cited a literal concern. The talk turns, as so often, to the issues of paying one's bills. But in a very Shakespearean way, the motif keeps edging into metaphor. In his first soliloquy, Hal speaks of his coming transformation: 'And pay the debt I never promised' (1.2.203). His system of personal conduct is an acknowledgement of debt. Hotspur, for his part, grounds his complaint against King Henry IV in his sense of debt repudiated:

> Revenge the jeering and disdain'd contempt
> Of this proud King, who studies day and night
> To answer all the debt he owes to you
> Even with the bloody payment of your deaths.

> (1.3.183–86)

At Hotspur sees it, the King has reneged on his obligations. History itself is absorbed into the morality of debt and repayment. And the idea continues to grow. The exchange between Hal and Falstaff before the battle of Shrewsbury makes *debt* the central metaphor for mortality:

> *Falstaff*   I would 'twere bed-time, Hal, and all well.
> *Prince*   Why, thou owest God a death. *[Exit]*
> *Falstaff*   'Tis not due yet; I would be loath to pay him
> before his day. What need I be so forward with
> him that calls not on me?

> (5.1.125–29)

There speaks the life force. Why pay one's debts before the due day? Clearly, the metaphoric range of the idea is very wide. It cannot be tethered on a short leash. But always the idea, in Part One more explicitly than in Part Two, comes down to the intellectual tension between two codes of conduct, Hal's and Falstaff's. The Prince's challenge to Douglas contains his motto-statement:

> It is the Prince of Wales that threatens thee,
> Who never promiseth but he means to pay.
>
> (5.4.42–43)

And Falstaff has nothing more characteristic than his response to Hal's 'The money is paid back again.' 'O, I do not like that paying back. 'Tis a double labour.' (3.3.178–80)

'Pay,' 'owe,' and 'debt' are central to the intellectual argument of *Henry IV*. The repeated situations and metaphors of debt and reckoning feed into our experience of the play, conditioning our minds to the deepest messages which the play sends. These messages are realized in the scenic alternation of pleasure and duty, the passages we endure in order to attain the passages we most enjoy.

––––––––––

In the scenes that embody our pleasure most deeply, locale is definitive. Of course, any scene with Falstaff will be fun; and he is fun on the road to Coventry as on the streets of London. But the true context for Falstaff is the tavern, and the tavern scenes. (That is 2.4 and 3.3. in Part One, 2.4 in Part Two.) Let us think about taverns.

The first point is that we *know* more about tavern life than any other area of English life in the first part of *Henry IV*. The textures of ordinary life are imparted with extraordinary density in the two great scenes, 2.4 and 3.3. David Bevington puts it well:

> The sense of locale for a tavern is created in the *Henry IV* plays not only by tables, stools, tapsters in their leather aprons, whores with their ruffs and jewels, 'lack-linen' swaggerers with swords and 'two points' on their shoulder, musicians, drinking companions with red countenances, talk of 'mouldy stew'd prunes and dried cakes,'

quantities of sack and the like (*2 Henry IV*, 2.4.122–145), but by a sense of enclosed space defined by two unseen presences, one the interior rooms of the tavern and the other the outside world.[2]

This 'interior room' is what we know most about. To this vital space is added the innyard, just outside. In the Rochester innyard scene (2.1), we learn of fleas, damp provender, staffing problems since the departure of the lamented Robin Ostler, the insanitary habits of the English, and the breakfast order of the travellers who 'call for eggs and butter.' The tavern, with its interior and its innyard, is the focus of life as it is lived. One could write an extended and no doubt largely accurate description of Elizabethan day-to-day realities simply on the basis of the tavern scenes. And it is symbolically apt that Hal, at the beginning of the great tavern scene, presents himself in the role of an observer come to study the linguistic and cultural ways of the English at their pleasures. 'I can drink with any tinker in his own language during my life.' (2.4.18–19) He seems a cultural anthropologist, a kind of reverse Fynes Moryson come from abroad to note the habitat and *mores* of this strange tribe, the English. He does it, and we could do it; the information is all there.

Note that we could accomplish nothing remotely comparable on the basis of the Court/rebel scenes. Their interest is human and political, but they are not embedded in the minutiae of everyday life. Technically, they are not so much thin as light, their context touched in with a few pencil strokes. It is the same principle as in *Twelfth Night*, where we could say a great deal about Olivia's household and very little about Orsino's court. The one locale stands out with stereoscopic intensity, the other is recessed and devoid of telling detail. Thus, the scenes in Part One which engage our emotions most profoundly are those which are rooted

in the real, in which there are innumerable physical en-
hancements of the authenticity of the experience.

Next, the tavern scenes are a defined type of room scene.
'The room', says Cirlot, 'is a symbol of individuality, of
private thoughts.'[3] That may not seem to describe closely
the tavern, with its multiple membership and sense of communal life. Nevertheless, the tavern is given over to the free
play of individuality. The tavern is the home of *homo ludens*,
man at ease with himself and his fellows. 'Shall I not take
mine ease in mine inn?' asks Falstaff (*1 Henry IV*, 3.3.81). In
this parenthesis of being, man is free to discover himself, to
enact himself as in a rehearsal. The room is also, as we see
in 2.4, an auditorium.

We can get a formal line on this tavern scene by calculating the geometry of Part One. Act Three, the middle act,
contains three scenes. The second scene (the private meeting between King Henry IV and the Prince of Wales) is
manifestly the scenic midpoint. As so often, Shakespeare
sets up a design in which 3.2 is the keystone of the arch.
That scene, 3.2, has 180 lines. We can therefore, in view of
Shakespeare's careful handling of mass and symmetry, look
with some confidence for the play's geographic centre to lie
at around line 91. In fact we find it at line 92. The Prince, in
answer to his father's tirade, has 'I shall hereafter, my thrice
gracious liege,/Be more myself.' (3.2.92–3) That self is in the
image of his kingly father: duty and authority. And where
did he learn of that self? In the Boar's Head, where the
freedom of the mimic games enabled him to change places
and roles with Falstaff. 'Dost thou speak like a king? Do
thou stand for me, and I'll play my father.' (2.4.428–29) The
self is a public one, triumphantly vindicated in Westminster
and on the fields of Shrewsbury and Agincourt. But that self
is first displayed in a private room in a tavern.

The tavern is also a refuge against the outside world.
Housman set his tavern against the tempest outside: 'The

doors clap to, the pane is blind with showers./Pass me the can, lad; there's an end of May.' Shakespeare's tavern is an enclosed world, where there is vast freedom to express oneself, but which is constantly under threat from without. It is, I think, a stage principle that all messages from outside are potentially threatening, if not actually so. (Pinter's *The Room* is the modern archetype.) They disturb at least the mood, if not the well-being of the actors.

We can see this principle illustrated in what is essentially though not formally a tavern scene, in *Twelfth Night* 2.3. The carousals of Sir Toby, Sir Andrew and Feste are first interrupted by Maria's warning, then closed down by the arrival of Malvolio. It is so with the tavern scene in *1 Henry IV*, 2.4. The Hostess comes to Hal with the news that 'there is a nobleman of the court at door would speak with you: he says he comes from your father.' (2.4.284–86) That is a cue, or call that the Prince chooses to ignore, or rather declassify: the message from father is to be converted to ridicule via Falstaff. 'Do thou stand for my father and examine me upon the particulars of my life.' (372–73) The impulse behind that speech is not so very different from Antony's reaction to an unwelcome message: 'Grates me: the sum.' At the end of the play episode comes *A knocking heard. Exeunt Hostess, Francis, and Bardolph. Enter Bardolph, running.* 'O, my lord, my lord, the sheriff with a most monstrous watch is at your door' (477–78). A few moments of agitated exchange pass, Falstaff and others make themselves scarce, then *Enter Sheriff and the Carrier.'* The party is over.

My point is that the mood is defined by the threat. Without this cold penetration from the outside world we would not understand so well the quality of being created inside the tavern. The prince does, after all, have to handle a police enquiry, one which concerns a genuine crime. The outside world insists on its right to re-define what, to the taverners, is a glorious and profitable prank. The later stages of this tavern scene might well be subtitled *An Inspector Calls.* This

outside world is illustrated in the Court, political, and military scenes: it is difficult, complex, often threatening, and
real. Moreover, it seeks to re-classify the tavern life as base,
unworthy, and aberrant. It is from that world that the
taverners take refuge. Hence the archetypal gesture of the
taverners is Falstaff's 'Hostess, clap to the doors!' (2.4.273)
and the archetypal threat is *knocking*.

We can get at the situation another way. Mark Rose remarks that

> Our responses as we watch Falstaff at his vocation can
> perhaps best be described in vitalist terms: after the nar-
> row, mechanical, constrained world of Francis and
> Hotspur in the first episode, we find ourselves in the
> presence of something organic and alive, and the effect is
> of release into sudden freedom.[4]

This 'release into sudden freedom' points to its pole, discipline and restraint. M. M. Mahood catches the implications
nicely: 'Falstaff, whose very charm lies in the way he repre-
sents freedom from all normal inhibitions, even succeeds in
breaking down those of the Lord Chief Justice, that walking
embodiment of Freud's Censor, to the point where he, too,
begins to pun.'[5] The contest between the life force and the
Censor has a first innings, Part One, in which the life force
has a clear lead. The second innings is a clear victory for the
Censor. That figure, the Lord Chief Justice, does not appear
in Part One; but his emissary, the Sheriff, does. The series of
interruptions to the life of the tavern, from Sir John Bracy
(the King's Messenger, intercepted by Falstaff) to the Sheriff
and Carrier, who are met but are not to be put off, points
towards the origin of the threats: King and Father, the Censor and the Law. It is from these forces that the taverners
shelter themselves.

The second tavern scene (3.3) makes the same points
more brusquely. The by-play with Hostess, Falstaff, and the

Prince is now a mere interlude which does not long hold up Hal's news: 'I have procur'd thee, Jack, a charge of foot.' (3.3.186) And Hal's talk is all of business: 'Go, Peto, to horse, to horse, for thou and I/Have thirty miles to ride yet ere dinner time.' (3.3.197–98) The tavern has now subtly changed its psychic map reference. From being firmly fixed in Eastcheap, it is a post-house on the road to Coventry. It is left to Falstaff to sound the note of regret and loss at the transformation:

> O, I could wish this tavern were my drum!

> (3.3.206)

To sum up so far. The tavern, as I maintain, is the setting for the most characteristic and inward scenes of Part One. The container for the pleasure principle, the tavern, is also the moral arena where the meaning of *pay, debt, owe,* and *reckoning* is established. In this arena the endless duel between Hal and Falstaff focuses the action. And all the time there plays upon the life of the tavern that draught from the outside world, the chill wind of war, business, affairs of State, a re-definition of experience. Beyond the tavern lies – to simplify the reference – the Court. The Court means something very different from what we habitually understand by it. It is not a graceful appendage to the real world, designer history, but the thing itself, the centre of power and State action. When Hal says 'I'll to the Court in the morning' (2.4.538), he means that he's going to work. Hal knows what Feste knows, 'Truly, sir, and pleasure will be paid, one time or another.' (*Twelfth Night*, 2.4.70–71) In this escape from Time and its cares the tavern is best seen as a version of pastoral.

Part Two also contains its tavern scene, also located at 2.4, but its emotional coloration is such that the Boar's Head no longer seems an urban pastoral. I am indebted to A. C. Sprague for a phrase which appeared in the *Leamington Spa Courier* of a local production: 'The Tavern Scene had been given "in all its hideous realism".'[6] This is the scene whose character-note is 'Peace, good Doll, do not speak like a death's head; do not bid me remember mine end' (232–33) and 'Is it not strange that desire should so many years outlive performance?' (259–60). The most Chekhovian scene in Shakespeare, I dare say, it is not one to give endless delight to an audience. The outcome of the contention between Time and the pleasure principle is no longer in balance; the Falstaffian life force is ebbing. The final *knocking* at the door is for Falstaff, and behind it is a larger summons.

So where does one look for the deepest pleasures of Part Two? Surely and always, to the Gloucestershire scenes at Shallow's home in the Cotswolds. (That is, Act 3 scene 3: Act 5, scenes 1 and 3.) I do not think that in this matter our experience will vary greatly from one production to another. It was of the famous Old Vic *Henry IV* of 1945 that Kenneth Tynan wrote: 'The most treasurable scenes in these two productions were those in Shallow's orchard: if I had only half an hour more to spend in theatres, and could choose at large, no question but I would have these.'[7] In that subtext of valediction, Tynan puts his finger on the enduring charm of the scenes. They are among other things our farewell to Falstaff. The Cotswolds are the scene of Falstaff's last great coup, a thousand-pound touch of his last major gull. The evening sun slants down on the apotheosis of Sir John, the great man playing on the provincial circuit after London is more or less closed down for him. It is a kind of anticipatory balm, switched in time from Act 6, when we would need it after the rejection of Falstaff, to the earlier part of Act 5. Hence I cannot accept R. W. David's view of the 'glorious irrelevancy of the Gloucestershire scenes.'[8]

The Cotswold scenes, above all the last one in Shallow's orchard, seem to me to contain the core of Part Two. The pastoral has moved from its urban container, the tavern, to its home. The rural idyll is actual and authentic. It is the realization of the green fields of which Falstaff, in his final act of self-definition, babbled.

Of the last scene (5.3), the most important feature is that it is a feast. Strictly, it is an aftermath to Shallow's feast, a late harvest, in which the eating and drinking continue outside the house. 'Nay, you shall see my orchard, where, in an arbour, we will eat a last year's pippin of mine own graffing, with a dish of caraways, and so forth . . .' (5.3.1–3) The feast is always for Shakespeare the great symbol of social accord, and none the less so because things so often go wrong in it. (*Macbeth, The Taming of the Shrew, Antony and Cleopatra*, for example.) This feast, until interrupted, has nothing wrong with it. Three old men and their followers sit out of doors on a warm evening, enjoying one another's company, drinking more sack, and listening with some surprise to the Songs of Silence.

> *Falstaff* I did not think Master Silence had been a man of this mettle.
>
> *Silence* Who, I? I have been merry twice and once ere now.
>
> (37–40)

Merry is the codeword for the early part of this scene. It occurs 14 times – but once only from Falstaff, who is, for him, fairly reserved. It is Silence who has 'An we shall be merry, now comes in the sweet o'th'night' (48–49), echoing Falstaff's words to Doll Tearsheet. This party has the authentic flavor of an occasion to which people are contributing unequally, and the gaiety comes primarily from Shallow and Silence. Whether Falstaff's is the reserve of repletion or melancholy the actor will have to decide.

When does this last supper take place? We ought to fix its position in the seasonal cycle, if it is possible. John Russell Brown argues for a spring festival:

> Several references in the text indicate that Shakespeare has imagined all this happening on an unexpectedly balmy afternoon in early Spring: the white wheat that stands through winter has been sown already, and the headlands are due to be sown with the red (or Spring) wheat; they have supped on mutton because the year's new lambs are not yet fattened; some pippins remain from last year's harvest.[9]

The Spring scenario doesn't fit the text too well. The reference to sowing the hade land with red wheat (5.1.13–15) fixes the time as August. Hinckley Fair and Stamford Fair were held in August as well as other occasions in the year. Also, Shallow speaks of the feast as 'supper' (5.3.14), which makes it the evening meal for the Elizabethans. It must be well after six o'clock when they move out into the orchard, and I find it hard to believe in 'an unexpectedly balmy afternoon in early Spring' when this is possible. The pippins might seem a problem, but I am advised that with the best storage conditions choice pippins might well be edible in August following the harvest. Shallow certainly has the air of one offering a choice delicacy, which his friends could by no means count upon receiving. I labour these points because I think it essential to get at the inwardness of the last scene in Shallow's orchard. The pastoral takes on the form of a late-summer feast where, under ideal but perfectly natural conditions, the old men can enjoy the last of the summer wine.

The experience seems an absolute, a haven of spiritual and physical well-being. And yet, just as in the earlier tavern scenes, the experience is defined by its threat. The rural idyll is under attack (as logically it must be) by the city, by

the very word 'London.' Shallow says it first, and the idyll
is beginning to fragment when Davy, a moment later, says
'I hope to see London once ere I die.' (60) That is the play's
warning, and the future is not long in arriving. It comes
with symbolic accuracy immediately after Shallow's injunction 'Lack nothing; be merry.' (69–70) 'Merry,' the word at
the core of the revels, yields to the stage direction which
editors interpolate at this point, *knocking*. They are entitled
to do this, because the next words, also spoken by Shallow,
are 'Look who's at door there, ho! Who knocks?' It is Pistol
who knocks, bearing like Marcade the news of the King's
death. As with *Love's Labour's Lost*, the tidings of mortality
disperse the summer revels.

———————

I have sought to bring out the underlying family likenesses
that bind the scenes of tavern and rural life. As I maintain,
these are the scenes that we respond to most deeply – and
look forward to, in the next production. They are the pleasure principle enthroned, and yet always about to be de-
throned. When in the first tavern scene Falstaff plays the
King, that is literally the enthronement of pleasure; but he
soon has to step down, and the Prince begins to learn how
to play his father. In the Cotswold scenes there is no place
for the Prince, and yet his coronation draws the revellers to
his Court. The symbolic manoeuvres of the authority figures, and those who would resist or replace them, give the
clue to the meaning of the tavern and Cotswold scenes.
Authority gets the last word in *Henry IV*, and its hard-won
victory is seen as inevitable and right. But it is not to the
authority figures that we turn, in our continued addiction to
the play. It is to those scenes in which pleasure is triumphant that we return, in memory as in playgoing. Through
the scenes in which pleasure and duty alternate, we learn
what it is that authority has to overcome, and what indeed
will not be overcome.

Notes

1: HAMLET'S DOUBLES

1. *The Doubling of Parts in Shakespeare's Plays* (London: Society for Theatre Research, 1966), p. 14.
2. Arthur Colby Sprague and J. C. Trewin, *Shakespeare's Plays Today: Customs and Conventions of the Stage* (Columbia, SC: University of South Carolina Press, 1971), p. 17.
3. William A. Ringler, Jr., 'The Number of Actors in Shakespeare's Early Plays,' in *The Seventeenth Century Stage*, ed. Gerald Eades Bentley (Chicago: University of Chicago Press, 1968), pp. 110–34.
4. *The Profession of Player in Shakespeare's Time* (Princeton, NJ: Princeton University Press, 1984), p. 229.
5. '"Form and Cause Conjoin'd": *Hamlet* and Shakespeare's Workshop,' *Shakespeare Survey 26* (1973), 11–20.
6. *The London Stage 1890–1899: A Calendar of Plays and Players*, 2 vols. (Metuchen, NJ: Scarecrow Press, 1976). Subsequent calendars for the London stage have been issued for 1900–1909, 2 vols. (1981); 1910–19, 2 vols. (1982); and 1920–29, 3 vols. (1984). The form used is the same throughout, and I treat it here as a composite work. In Wearing's system, the first two digits refer to the date. 09:14 means the fourteenth production listed for 1909.
7. *Theatre at Stratford-upon-Avon: A Catalogue-Index to Productions of the Shakespeare Memorial/Royal Shakespeare Theatre, 1879–1978*, compiled and edited by Michael Mullin with Karen Morris Muriello, 2 vols. (Westport, Conn.: Greenwood Press, 1980).
8. The exceptional textual accuracy of the speeches for these four parts seems almost certain to indicate that a single actor, playing all four parts, was the source for the First Quarto edition. This assumption is widely accepted, as in Harold Jenkins's New Arden edition of *Hamlet* (London: Methuen, 1982), pp. 20–21. But Ringler is startlingly certain that 'the two parts cannot be doubled.' Ringler, p. 127.
9. Sprague, Appendix, p. 35.
10. Bernard Crick, *The Times Higher Educational Supplement*, 13 February 1976.
11. *Hamlet and Oedipus* (New York: W. W. Norton, 1949), p. 90.
12. *The Times*, 11 December 1975.
13. *Plays and Players*, February 1976.
14. *Shakespeare Quarterly*, 28 (1977), 184. Richard David notes the double without offering an interpretation in *Shakespeare in the Theatre* (Cambridge: Cambridge University Press, 1978), pp. 78–79.

15. *Daily Telegraph*, 29 April 1966. The Ghost is described in David Addenbrooke, *The Royal Shakespeare Company* (London: William Kimber, 1974), p. 131; and Stanley Wells, *Royal Shakespeare: Four Productions at Stratford-upon-Avon* (Manchester: Manchester University Press, 1977), p. 34.
16. See Peter Thomson, 'A Necessary Theatre: The Royal Shakespeare Season 1970 Reviewed,' *Shakespeare Survey 24* (1971), 123.
17. *The Property Basket* (London: Collins & Harvill Press, 1970), p. 60.
18. 22 April 1920.
19. Bladon Peake, *Stratford-upon-Avon Herald*, 3 August 1928.
20. *Birmingham Gazette*, 27 April 1929.
21. 27 April 1922.
22 Charles Lewsen, 'In various directions,' *Plays and Players*, October 1982, 13.
23. *The Listener*, 4 April 1980.
24. Colin Ludlow, *Plays and Players*, May 1980, 25–26.
25. Ludlow, 25–26.

2: DOUBLING: THEORY AND PRACTICE

1. A. C. Sprague lists many examples of the once-popular Ghost/Laertes double in the appendix to *The Doubling of Parts in Shakespeare's Plays* (London: Society for Theatre Research, 1966). Gary Jay Williams disposes briskly of a recent directorial coupling of Falstaff and Henry IV, heterogeneous ideas yoked by violence together: 'Shakespeare in Washington, D.C.,' *Shakespeare Quarterly*, 36 (1985), 463–68.
2. *Theatre at Stratford-upon-Avon: A Catalogue-Index to Productions of the Shakespeare Memorial/Royal Shakespeare Theatre, 1879–1978*, compiled and edited by Michael Mullin with Karen Morris Muriello, 2 vols. (Westport, Conn.: Greenwood Press, 1980), 0880 and 0882.
3. *The London Stage 1920–1929: A Calendar of Plays and Players* by J. P. Wearing, 3 vols. (Metuchen, NJ: Scarecrow Press, 1984), 25.290.
4. 11 October 1925.
5. 8 October 1925. The *Observer* reviewer made the same point that Wardwell 'was good in the widely different parts which he doubled, the dying Edward IV and the victorious Richmond.' 11 October 1925.
6. 'Cordelia and the Fool,' *Shakespeare Quarterly*, 12 (1961), 127–32.
7. 'The practice of doubling and its influence on early dramaturgy', in *Pre-Restoration Stage Studies* (Cambridge, Mass.: Harvard University Press, 1927), pp. 43–78, 72–73.
8. 'Shakespeare and his Actors: Some Remarks on *King Lear*' in *Shakespeare's Art from a Comparative Perspective*, ed. Wendell M. Aycock (Lubbock: Texas Technological University Press, 1981), pp. 183–94.

9. *Shakespeare's Clown: Actor and Text in the Elizabethan Playhouse* (Cambridge: Cambridge University Press, 1987), pp. 144–158.
10. Letter dated 13 March 1950.
11. There is a single instance known to me, the *Cymbeline* directed by a four-man collective (Braham Murray, Greg Hersov, James Maxwell, Casper Wrede) at the Royal Exchange, Manchester, in 1984. Hugh Quarshie's double of Cloten and Posthumus rather gravelled the reviewers, of whom Anthony Masters is representative: 'Now Hugh Quarshie is black, which might have served to emphasize Posthumus's underprivileged position in society – were it not that he is also playing a King's pampered brat.' *The Times*, 14 September 1984.
12. 'Cloten, Autolycus and Caliban: Bearers of Parodic Burdens,' in *Shakespeare's Romances Reconsidered*, ed. Carol McGinnis Kay and Henry E. Jacobs (Lincoln, Nebr.: University of Nebraska Press, 1978), pp. 100–1.
13. See my *Shakespearean Structures* (London: Macmillan, 1981), pp. 129–32.
14. Many instances are listed in Sprague, *op. cit.*
15. Interview with Ronald Hayman, *The Times*, 29 August 1970.
16. *The Times*, 28 August 1970.
17. *New Statesman*, 4 September 1970.
18. 'Free Shakespeare,' *Shakespeare Survey 24* (1971), 133.
19. *Stage Images and Traditions: Shakespeare to Ford* (Cambridge: Cambridge University Press, 1987), p. 87. For Declan Donnellan's comments on his *Pericles* doubling, see my *On Directing Shakespeare: Interviews with Contemporary Directors* (London: Hamish Hamilton, 1989), p. 202.
20. 'The Transmission of *Pericles*,' *Papers of the Bibliographical Society of America*, 80 (1986), 193–217.
21. Denis Bartholomeusz says that the double goes back to the famous Lyceum production of 1887, when Mary Anderson played Perdita and Hermione to great acclaim. *'The Winter's Tale' in Performance in England and America 1611–1976* (Cambridge: Cambridge University Press, 1982), pp. 116–22.
22. *The Times*, 3 April 1969.
23. *Financial Times*, 3 April 1969.
24. *New Statesman*, 11 April 1969.
25. Ronald Hastings, 'A New Conception of *Pericles*,' *Daily Telegraph*, 29 March 1969.
26. *Sunday Times*, 6 April 1969.
27. The full cast is listed in Mullin, *Theatre at Stratford-upon-Avon*, 0808.
28. The programme has on its cover a quotation from Plato's *Symposium*, beginning 'After the division the two parts of man, each desiring his other half, came together, and throwing their arms about one another, entwined in mutual embraces . . .'

3: CASTING THE CHORUS

1. William Arrowsmith, 'Chorus,' in *Princeton Encyclopedia of Poetry and Poetics*, ed. Alex Preminger, Frank J. Warnke and O. B. Hardison, Jr. (Princeton, NJ: Princeton University Press, 1965).

2. *The New York Times*, 4 June 1966. The most extensive and penetrating review of the production is by John Pettigrew, in 'Stratford's Festival Theatre: 1966,' *Queen's Quarterly*, 73 (1966).

3. 'A Stratford Production: *Henry VIII*,' *Shakespeare Survey* 3 (1950), 120–29, 121.

4. The production is reviewed in my 'Resurgence at Stratford,' *Queen's Quarterly*, 93 (1986), 750–59.

5. In the most recent RSC production, 1984, Howard Davies ducked the choice by assigning Prologue's lines to Henry (the amiable Richard Griffiths).

6. *The Broken Heart* by John Ford, ed. T. J. B. Spencer (London: Methuen, 1980), p. 14.

7. Denis Bartholomeusz, *'The Winter's Tale' in Performance in England and America 1611–1976* (Cambridge: Cambridge University Press, 1982), p. 43.

8. Ibid., p.92.

9. *Theatre at Stratford-upon-Avon: A Catalogue-Index to Productions of the Shakespeare Memorial/Royal Shakespeare Theatre, 1879–1978*, compiled and edited by Michael Mullin with Karen Morris Muriello, 2 vols. (Westport, Conn.: Greenwood Press, 1980), p. 1180.

10. Bartholomeusz, op. cit., p. 207.

11. Ibid., p. 213.

12. Ibid.

13. Ibid., p. 222.

14. Richard David, *Shakespeare in the Theatre* (Cambridge: Cambridge University Press, 1978), p. 222.

15. Terry Hands's RSC production of 1986 merits only a footnote. 'I must confess to being a trifle startled when Time . . . arrives as an untidy-winged creature who addresses us in the accents of Churdles Ash,' was J. C. Trewin's reaction (*Birmingham Post*, 1 May 1986). David Ford saw 'a grotesque Time who flies aloft in a somewhat tatty seagull uniform' (*Worcester Evening News*, 1 May 1986).

16. Christopher Marlowe, *Doctor Faustus: The A-Text*, ed. David Ormerod and Christopher Wortham (Nedlands, Western Australia: University of Western Australia Press, 1985), 815.2–826.

17. Ormerod and Wortham, p. 84.

18. W. W. Greg, *Marlowe's 'Doctor Faustus'* (Oxford: Clarendon Press, 1950), p. 60.

19. E. K. Chambers, *The Elizabethan Stage*, 4 vols. (Oxford: Clarendon Press, 1923), ii. 547.

20. Christopher Marlowe, *Doctor Faustus*, ed. John D. Jump (London: Methuen, 1962), sc.xx lines 18–19.

21. See Robert Speaight, *William Poel and the Elizabethan Revival* (London: Heinemann, 1954), pp. 113–19. Shaw reviewed the production, without however commenting on Chorus. *Our Theatres in the Nineties*, 3 vols. (London: Constable, 1932), ii. 181–86.
22. *The Observer*, 1 September 1974.
23. *Daily Telegraph*, 9 September 1974.
24. *New Statesman*, 13 September 1974.
25   *The Times*, 12 May 1989.
26   *Observer*, 14 May 1989. There was no clear link between Wagner and the production's meaning. 'Richard McCabe plays him as a sombre joker,' wrote John Peter (*The Sunday Times*, 14 May 1989).
27. Margaret Ingram, *Stratford-upon-Avon Herald* (24 July 1987).

4: CASTING THE CROWD:
CORIOLANUS IN PERFORMANCE

1. Chorus in *Henry V* apologizes for presenting Agincourt 'with four or five most vile and ragged foils.'
2. Julian Charles Young, from *A Memoir of Charles Mayne Young, Tragedian*. Quoted in Gareth Lloyd Evans, *Shakespeare in the Limelight* (Glasgow and London: Blackie, 1968), p. 66.
3. 'Kemble made no open attempt to focus the play on the politics of the Europe of his time.' J. P. Brockbank, in the New Arden edition of *Coriolanus* (London: Methuen, 1976), p. 80. It may well be queried whether, in 1789, Kemble dared make the point that history was making for him.
4. *John Bull*, 19 March 1838. Quoted by George C. D. Odell, *Shakespeare from Betterton to Irving*, 2 vols. (New York: Scribner, 1920), ii. 212–13.
5. Alan Hughes, *Henry Irving, Shakespearean* (Cambridge: Cambridge University Press, 1981), p. 167.
6. April 1901.
7. See J. P. Wearing, *The London Stage 1910–1919: A Calendar of Plays and Players*, 2 vols. (Metuchen, NJ: Scarecrow Press, 1982); and *The London Stage 1920–1929: A Calendar of Plays and Players*, 3 vols. (Metuchen, NJ: Scarecrow Press, 1984). The Old Vic production was in 1920, listed under 20.114.
8. A. P. Rossiter, *Angel With Horns* (London: Longman, 1961), p. 237.
9. Kenneth Tynan, *Curtains* (New York: Atheneum, 1961), p. 240.
10. Kenneth Hurren, *Theatre Inside Out* (London: W. H. Allen, 1977), p. 70.
11. Robert Cushman, *Plays and Players* (July 1971), 34, 59.
12. Irving Wardle, *The Times* (13 April 1967). And: 'Coriolanus is not a political figure at all, but an aristocrat who reckons that it is his right to rule the people if he wants to . . .' B. A. Young, *Financial Times* (13 April 1967).

13. Frank Cox, *Plays and Players* (June 1972), 36.
14. Carol A. Chillington, *Educational Theatre Journal* (May 1978), 258–59.
15. David Daniell, *'Coriolanus' in Europe* (London: Athlone Press, 1980), 59.
16. Ibid., 60, 70, 107–8, 139–40.
17. Ibid., 21.
18. Benedict Nightingale, *New Statesman* (21 December 1984).
19. Francis King, *Sunday Telegraph* (23 December 1984).
20. Michael Ratcliffe, *Observer* (23 December 1984).
21. Michael Billington, *Guardian* (17 December 1984).
22. Michael Coveney, *Financial Times* (17 December 1984).
23. Steve Grant, *Time Out* (3 January 1985).
24. Milton Shulman, *Standard* (17 December 1984).
25. Laurence Kitchin, *Mid-Century Drama* (London: Faber, 1960), p. 140.
26. Terry Hands's production of *Coriolanus* (RSC, 1989–90), offers a footnote but no change of direction. Sheridan Morley's judgment of Charles Dance's Coriolanus is fair: 'he is forced to give a scar-faced performance of considerable strength and interest in a stage vacuum. And, in the end, his stardom is just not enough to see us through a lengthy evening of flat lighting and non-committal support.' *International Herald Tribune*, 9 May 1990.

5: CASTING HAMLET: TWO TRADITIONS

1. Christopher Edwards, *New Statesman*, 19 August 1982.
2. John A. Mills, *'Hamlet' on Stage: the Great Tradition* (Westport,Conn.: Greenwood Press, 1985), p. 263.
3. 'Branagh gives off an air of healthy well-being.' Christopher Edwards, *Spectator*, 17 September 1988.
4. *Times Higher Education Supplement*, 13 February 1976.
5. *Royal Shakespeare: Four Major Productions at Stratford-upon-Avon* (Manchester: Manchester University Press, 1977), p. 33. This comes from the fullest and best account of the Warner/Hall *Hamlet*, pp. 23–42.
6. Peter Hall, 'Director in Interview,' *Plays and Players* (June 1970). Quoted in David Addenbrooke, *The Royal Shakespeare Company* (London: William Kimber, 1974), p. 129.
7. 'The Royal Shakespeare Company 1965,' *Shakespeare Survey 19* (1966), 113.
8. Mills, op. cit., 265.
9. 'Shakespeare in Britain,' *Shakespeare Quarterly*, 17 (1966), 394.
10. *The Times*, 18 February 1969.
11. Mills, op. cit., 268.
12. Eric Shorter, *Daily Telegraph*, 23 May 1984.
13. Jack Tinker, *Daily Mail*, 29 May 1984.
14. Rosalie Horner, *Daily Express*, 18 August 1982.
15. Steve Grant, *Time Out*, 29 November 1989.

16. Della Couling, *Tablet*, 27 June 1987.
17. *Punch*, 24 June 1987.
18. *Guardian*, 12 June 1987.
19. *A View of the English Stage* (London: Davis-Poynter, 1975), p. 21.
20. See my *On Directing Shakespeare: Interviews with Contemporary Directors*, second edition (London: Hamish Hamilton, 1989), p. 38.

6: LEAR'S SYSTEM AND CORDELIA'S ASIDE: LEADING THE AUDIENCE

1. George Orwell, 'Lear, Tolstoy, and the Fool,' in *Selected Essays* (Harmondsworth: Penguin, 1957), p. 116.
2. Kenneth Muir, New Arden edition of *King Lear* (London: Methuen, 1964), p. liii.
3. G. Wilson Knight, *The Wheel of Fire* (London: Methuen, 1930), p. 162.
4. A. C. Bradley, *Shakespearean Tragedy* (London: Macmillan, 1904), p. 232.
5. Elder Olson, *Tragedy and the Theory of Drama* (Detroit: Wayne State University Press, 1961), p. 201.
6. Winifred Nowottny, 'Some Aspects of the Style of *King Lear*,' *Shakespeare Survey 13* (1960), 53.
7. Peter Brook, *The Empty Space* (London: MacGibbon & Kee, 1968), p. 14.
8. See Richard David's *Shakespeare in the Theatre* (Cambridge: Cambridge University Press, 1978), pp. 95–105; and my reviews of the Stratford, Ontario seasons, 'Stratford Festival Canada,' in *Shakespeare Quarterly*, 31 (1980), 167–75, and 32 (1981), 176–80.
9. *King Lear: A New Variorum Edition*, ed. H. H. Furness (New York, 1880).
10. Bradley, op. cit., p. 211.
11. 'Behind the façade of unanimity, all dictatorships are to a large extent centrifugal: the rule of a court conceals a political anarchy in which jealous feudatories, with private armies and reservations of public resources, are secretly bargaining, and may openly fight, for the reversion or preservation of power.' Hugh Trevor-Roper, *The Last Days of Hitler* (New York: Macmillan, 1947), p. 233.
12. E. A. J. Honigmann, *Shakespeare: Seven Tragedies: The Dramatist's Manipulation of Response* (London: Macmillan, 1978), p. 103.
13. Bradley, op. cit., p. 265.
14. Most notably in Maynard Mack, *'King Lear' in Our Time* (Berkeley and Los Angeles: University of California Press, 1965). But the later scholarly view of the Folio as a fully revised text makes Mack's strictures look much less telling. If Shakespeare could cut the post-blinding dialogue in his revision, why not Brook?

15. Bradley, op. cit., p. 264.
16. John Dover Wilson, *King Lear*, New Cambridge edition (Cambridge: Cambridge University Press, 1960), p. xx.
17. It is worth noting, though, that 4.3, with the Gentleman's description of Cordelia, disappears in what we are now to think of as the Folio revision. Those who wish to make much of Cordelia's 'holy water' and 'heavenly eyes' must reconcile themselves to the willed departure of those pointers.

7: LAUGHTER IN *KING RICHARD II:* THE SUBPLOT OF MOOD

1. *Stage Directions* (London: Heinemann, 1963), p. 30.
2. Ibid., p. 31.
3. *Shakespeare's Histories* (London: Society for Theatre Research, 1964), p. 42.
4. *Royal Shakespeare* (Manchester: Manchester University Press, 1976), p. 74.
5. Ibid.
6. *Going to Shakespeare* (London: George Allen & Unwin, 1978), pp. 87, 89.
7. 'Aumerle's Conspiracy,' *Studies in English Literature 1500–1900* (Spring 1974), 239–57.
8. *Going to Shakespeare*, p. 83.
9. J. C. Trewin, *Shakespeare on the English Stage 1900–1964* (London: Barrie & Rockliff, 1964), p. 207. The production was at the New Theatre, London, 1947.
10. Eric Shorter, *Daily Telegraph* (12 September 1986). Irons starred in Barry Kyle's RSC production of 1986.
11. *Guardian*, 12 September 1986.
12. *The Times*, 12 September 1986.
13. Poel embraced this truth. 'William Poel conceived of the Duke of York as a comic character and saw to it that he was so represented in the production of *Richard II* by the Elizabethan Stage Society.' A. C. Sprague, *Shakespeare's Histories*, p. 41.
14. 'Repetition overdone or not going anywhere belongs to comedy, for laughter is partly a reflex, and like other reflexes it can be conditioned by a simple repeated pattern.' Northrop Frye, *Anatomy of Criticism* (Princeton: Princeton University Press, 1957), p. 168.
15. *Going to Shakespeare*, p. 87.
16. 24 March 1951.
17. *Daily Telegraph*, 26 March 1951.
18. *Scotsman*, 17 April 1964.
19. John Barber, *Daily Telegraph*, 4 November 1980.
20. *Financial Times*, 4 November 1980.

21. *The Times*, 12 September 1986.
22. *Financial Times*, 12 September 1986.
23. *Daily Telegraph*, 12 September 1986.
24. *Going to Shakespeare*, p. 87.

8: METAMORPHOSES OF THE AUDIENCE

1. Bernard Beckerman emphasizes the need for the 'ranking figure' to act as the central point of reference in group scenes, whatever staging is adopted. This principle must have been invaluable in Elizabethan rehearsals. *Shakespeare at the Globe 1599–1609* (New York: Macmillan, 1962), pp. 170–71.
2. Richard A. Levin, *Love and Society in Shakespearean Comedy* (Newark, NJ: University of Delaware Press, 1985), pp. 69–78.
3. Richard E. Mennen, 'Theodore Komisarjevsky's Production of *The Merchant of Venice*', *Theatre Journal* 31 (1979), 386–97.

9: DRAMATIS PERSONAE

1. *William Shakespeare: The Complete Works*, ed. Stanley Wells and Gary Taylor (Oxford: Oxford University Press, 1986).
2. *The Riverside Shakespeare*, ed. G. Blakemore Evans (Boston: Houghton Mifflin, 1974); *The Complete Works of Shakespeare*, ed. David Bevington, third edition (Glenview, Ill.: Scott, Foresman, 1980). The New Arden series (London: Methuen) began in 1951; the Oxford and New Cambridge single-text series began in 1984.
3. *An Index to 'The Elizabethan Stage' and 'William Shakespeare' by Sir Edmund Chambers* compiled by Beatrice White (Oxford: Clarendon Press, 1934) contains no reference to dramatis personae. I cannot discover significant coverage of the topic in the works of W. W. Greg, F. T. Bowers, and Stanley Wells on editing Shakespeare. There are some useful pages in E. A. J. Honigmann, *The Stability of Shakespeare's Text* (Lincoln, Nebr.: University of Nebraska Press, 1965), pp. 38, 44 ff.
4. Bevington, the Riverside, and the New Arden (1981) make the reader wait until 3.5 for the footnote that explains 'headborough.'
5. *Twelfth Night*, p. 2.
6. E. A. J. Honigmann argues that 'somewhere in Act II Shakespeare abandoned his plans for Montano, the build-up for which he had already commenced.' Honigmann, op. cit., p. 39.
7. Terry Hands, quoted in Sally Beauman (ed.), *The Royal Shakespeare Company Centenary Production of 'Henry V'* (Oxford: Pergamon, 1976), p. 79.

10: *MEASURE FOR MEASURE:* CASTING THE STAR

1. Michael Redgrave tells how he persuaded Tyrone Guthrie to change his offer from Horatio to Laertes. 'Laertes by all means if you prefer, though *I'd* call Horatio the better part.' Michael Redgrave, *In My Mind's Eye* (London: Weidenfeld & Nicolson, 1983), p. 96.
2. Ralph Berry, *On Directing Shakespeare: Interviews with Contemporary Directors* (London: Hamish Hamilton, 1989), pp. 167–68.
3. 10 March 1950.
4. 10 March 1950.
5. 10 March 1950.
6. 14 August 1956.
7. 15 August 1956.
8. *Daily Telegraph*, 15 August 1956.
9. Ibid.
10. 15 August 1956.
11. Jane Williamson, 'The Duke and Isabella on the Modern Stage,' in *The Triple Bond: Plays, Mainly Shakespearean, in Performance*, ed. Joseph G. Price (University Park and London: Pennsylvania State University Press, 1975), pp. 149–69.
12. *Financial Times*, 11 April 1962.
13. 11 April 1962.
14. *Birmingham Post*, 11 April 1962.
15. *Guardian*, 11 April 1962.
16. Irving Wardle, *The Times*, 2 April 1970.
17. Michael Billington, *Guardian*, 5 September 1974.
18. Irving Wardle, *The Times*, 5 September 1974.
19. Hilary Spurling, *Observer*, 8 September 1974.
20. Richard David, *Shakespeare in the Theatre* (Cambridge: Cambridge University Press, 1978), p. 9.
21. Irving Wardle, *The Times*, 14 August 1975.
22. Ibid.
23. *Birmingham Post*, 28 June 1978.
24. *The Times*, 5 October 1983.
25. *Evesham Journal*, 13 October 1983.
26. 14 October 1983.
27. Michael Bogdanov's thinking on *Measure for Measure* can be gleaned from an extensive review of his production at Stratford, Ontario, in 1985. In it he cast two leading Canadian actors, Alan Scarfe and Nicholas Pennell, as the Duke and Angelo, with the focus on the Duke. See Herbert S. Weil, Jr., 'Stratford Festival Canada,' *Shakespeare Quarterly* 37 (1986), 245–50.
28. *Daily Telegraph*, 13 November 1987.

11: WITHIN THE BERMUDA TRIANGLE: REFLECTIONS ON RECENT *TEMPESTS*

1. Constance Benson, *Mainly Players: Bensonian Memories* (London: Thornton Butterworth, 1926), p. 179. F. R. Benson saw Caliban as the missing link, an interpretation stemming from Daniel Wilson's *Caliban: The Missing Link* (Toronto, 1873). There is a useful treatment of the Darwinian Caliban in Virginia Mason Vaughan, '"Something rich and strange:" Caliban's Theatrical Metamorphoses,' *Shakespeare Quarterly*, 36 (1985), 390–405.
2. Milton Shulman, *Standard*, 14 September 1983.
3. Jonathan Miller openly read *The Tempest* in terms of *Prospero and Caliban* (second edition, New York: Praeger, 1964), Ottave Mannoni's study of the French colonial experience in Madagascar. See Ralph Berry, *On Directing Shakespeare: Interviews with Contemporary Directors* (London: Hamish Hamilton, 1989), pp. 33–35. See also Patrick Marnham's obituary of Mannoni in *The Independent* (2 August 1989).
4. David Suchet, 'Caliban,' in *Players of Shakespeare*, ed. J. P. Brockbank (Cambridge: Cambridge University Press, 1985), pp. 167–79.
5. Ibid., p. 169.
6. Ibid., p. 179.
7. A photograph is reproduced in Stephen Orgel's edition of *The Tempest* (Oxford: Oxford University Press, 1987), p. 82.
8. Berry, op. cit., p. 200.
9. Braham Murray's production of *The Tempest* at the Royal Exchange, Manchester, strikes me as an accurate barometric reading of the contemporary Caliban. '. . . there is an engaging performance as Caliban from Dan Hildebrand. With his rags, Rasta-style locks and gaudy tattoos, he might be a cross between some alienated North London squatter and the Cowardly Lion in the *Wizard of Oz*. It is possible to see both why Caliban looks for a leader when planning violence, and why Prospero keeps him chained. There is something both feeble and feral about his hooliganism.' Benedict Nightingale, *The Times*, 15 September 1990.
10. *The Tempest*, ed. Orgel, p. 70.
11. It is reproduced in Rachel Kempson [Lady Redgrave], *Life Among the Redgraves* (New York: Dutton, 1988). See also the photograph of Elsa Lanchester as Ariel to Charles Laughton's Prospero at the Old Vic, 1934. *The Tempest*, ed. Orgel, p. 78.
12. The sexual view, as revealed in the costuming, defies generalization. But it may be worth recalling Robert Hardy's admission that he played Ariel clad only in 'a kind of genital sunburst.'
13. Irving Wardle, *The Times*, 21 May 1988.
14. *The Times*, 29 July 1988.
15. *Peter Hall's Diaries*, ed. John Goodwin (London: Hamish Hamilton, 1983), p. 12.

12: FALSTAFF'S SPACE:
THE TAVERN AS PASTORAL

1. J. C. Trewin, *Going to Shakespeare* (London: George Allen & Unwin, 1978), p. 113.
2. David Bevington, *Action is Eloquence: Shakespeare's Language of Gesture* (Cambridge, Mass. and London: Harvard University Press, 1984), p. 132.
3. J. F. Cirlot, *A Dictionary of Symbols* (New York: Philosophical Library, 1962), p. 262.
4. Mark Rose, *Shakespearean Design* (Cambridge, Mass.: Harvard University Press, 1972), p. 53.
5. M. M. Mahood, *Shakespeare's Wordplay* (London: Methuen, 1957), p. 29.
6. A. C. Sprague, *Shakespeare's Histories* (London: Society for Theatre Research, 1964), p. 74.
7. Kenneth Tynan, *He Who Plays The King* (London: Longmans, Green, 1950), p. 51.
8. R. W. David, 'Shakespeare's History Plays – Epic or Drama?', *Shakespeare Survey 6* (1953), 137.
9. John Russell Brown, *Discovering Shakespeare: A New Guide to the Plays* (London: Macmillan, 1981), p. 153.

Index